BRITAIN
IN OLD PHOTOGRAPHS

POULTON, THORNTON & BISPHAM

CATHERINE ROTHWELL

SUTTON PUBLISHING

Sutton Publishing Limited
Phoenix Mill · Thrupp · Stroud
Gloucestershire · GL5 2BU

First published 2002

Title-page photograph: Mr Bulmer, the postman from Sheaf Street, on his rounds by a VR box at Thistleton, 1893. Penny postage was a blessing but mail went astray so the clerk of the magistrates decided to add le-Fylde to Poulton's name. There was another Poulton which later became Morecambe.

British Library Cataloguing in Publication Data
A catalogue record for this book is available from the British Library.

ISBN 0-7509-2952-9

Typeset in 10.5/13.5 Photina.
Typesetting and origination by
Sutton Publishing Limited.
Printed and bound in England by
J.H. Haynes & Co. Ltd, Sparkford.

A Lomas grandfather clock, 1967. Samuel and Richard Lomas, father and son, made grandfather clocks in Poulton in the second half of the eighteenth century. They lived at what is now 16 Hardhorn Road, Sheaf Street as was. There are entries in the St Chad's churchwarden's vestry book referring to the Lomases mending the church clock.

CONTENTS

Yates's eighteenth-century map of the old Fylde (Amounderness). Note 'Mr Forshaw's Bathing Place', later Blackpool, on the left just above centre. (*Lancashire Record Office*)

INTRODUCTION

Poulton-le-Fylde has the most complete example of its kind in England of a market cross, stocks, fish stones and whipping post. Such was the proud boast in the eighteenth and nineteenth centuries when visitors were taking a greater interest in the past and people like Charles Dickens, John Bright and Keir Hardie were asking questions as they passed through. Then why did a group of councillors decide to knock down the medieval tithe barn in the late 1960s? You may well ask this good question for, with hindsight, this was a unique building, where corn was threshed, tithes honoured, plays staged and, for a short time, church services held. With its close proximity to the ancient Parish Church of St Chad, this could have been the jewel in Poulton's crown.

However, in spite of the changes, most of them necessary, Poulton has not lost all its links with the past. Amid its compact pattern of streets there are reminders. At the top of Breck Road (breck is old Norse for gentle slope) look up at the red-brick Ship Inn. The sailing ship in carved terracotta denotes that Poulton was once a port, with vessels plying to Russia and the West Indies. Emigrants sailed from Skippool Creek, slaves were delivered and Wardleys was a legal quay. A century and a half ago there was a model of a clipper ship swinging in the wind above the inn door. Sailors put up in Potts Alley (now Chapel Court) and a merry time they had between voyages at the fifteen inns that were located in twelve streets. The Thatched House Inn was, indeed, thatched and half-timbered. The aroma of coffee wafting from today's Corn Mill Café hints at the fact that a large corn mill, several storeys high, once stood in that vicinity.

Important horse sales were held in Market Place. Stalls were piled high with provender of every kind, including piglets in crates and live geese, especially at Christmas. From all the country around, farmers converged on the River Wyre ford and there was cart rage in the race to beat tides – to arrive early for market day in the 'metropolis of the Fylde' was essential.

The bells of St Chad rang out at the victories of the Nile and Trafalgar. The pancake bell clanged every Shrove Tuesday at 11 a.m., eagerly pulled by an apprentice to start the other apprentices running up and down the village demanding pancakes. The curfew bell was obligatory between the months of October and March. 'Couvre feu' – 'protect your fire' – was a necessary warning in a village constructed from wood and thatch. In Poulton, funerals were customary at night, especially for important people. A flaming torch once destroyed the entire west side of Market Place.

It must have been a spectacle when the 'yard of tin', echoing from far off, heralded the approach of the mail coaches. Timing was of the essence, unless held up by flood or snow, in which case the post boy unhitched the lead horse and galloped ahead with the mail bag to the Bull or the Golden Ball. No respecter of persons, the coachman carried all before him, upheld by the law.

In the early nineteenth century, the areas of Thornton and Bispham were described by Canon St Vincent Beechey and Captain William Latham when he sailed and sketched the River Wyre.

The great house of the lord of the manor looked out on a small community of whitewashed buildings, beyond which rolled acres of treeless pasture broken only by small farms. Most of the land, less than 25 ft above sea level and buffeted by prevailing westerly winds, was frequently flooded by the sea. Marram grass covered the sandhills, which were starred with sea pinks, sea holly, sea lavender and evening primrose. The main inhabitants were rabbits, herring gulls and oyster catchers in their thousands. Starkly against what Latham calls 'the Northern Mountains' rose the old wooden landmark. There was a wealth of fish in the sea and many a Bispham, Thornton, Norbreck and Angersholme man went fishing, musseling and cockling. John Thornber described what could be found on the shore: '[sea shells] pink and lilac in colour, pearly trochuses, sea worms, sea urchins, all kinds of seaweed'. Inland the flatness of the horizon was punctuated by Bourne Hall built on a drumlin and the tower of Marsh Mill. Beyond the wastes of Thornton Marsh loomed the steel-blue hulk of Bleasdale Fells.

Thornton was recorded in the Domesday Book as being celebrated for oats and corn. In the eighteenth century grain was conveyed by packhorses to markets in Poulton and Preston. Tied on a wooden saddle, the load was fixed firmly by a wantah (a local word meaning a long leather strap wrapped around an animal and its load). The leading horse was fitted with a bell and the team following became so familiar with the route that the drover left them to find their way back to Thornton while he bargained over the load delivered.

Under the Marsh Act Award of 1805 Bold Fleetwood Hesketh built the high bank of gravel over Thornton Marsh to keep the sea off fertile land. His Ramper Road became Victoria Road, but at the equinox the sea still reached Parr's Lane, now Meadows Avenue.

Old Clevelas contained little more than the Cleveleys Hotel where landlord Robert Hindle was instrumental in saving the crew of the New Brunswick barque *Abana* in December 1894. He sent a lad off on horseback to alert the Blackpool lifeboat. During that storm eight vessels were wrecked in Morecambe Bay, an oyster stall flew on to the roof of Blackpool Central station, haystacks were scattered and the sails of Marsh Mill were badly damaged.

As the century advanced and Thornton became Thornton-Cleveleys, thatched cottages there and in Bispham became shops – 'Mr Shawcross, high class confectioner; Robert Hodgson, barber and tobacconist "dealer in English and foreign cigars"; W.E. Bailey, fruiterer and greengrocer'. A Bispham herbalist sold worm powder, nerve powder, fever cure, indigestion mixture and stomach bitters. The 'nine days' wonder', a recipe for beef and malt wine, also originated in Bispham:

> *1 pint of old port wine*
> *1 ounce of beef extract*
> *4 ounces of malt extract*
> *Mix: keep well corked for seven days*
> *occasionally shaking. Drink*

I have not tried it and am unsure what it was supposed to cure. I still chuckle when I think of the true story told to me by an octogenarian resident of the town about a Poulton shop. There had been 'fireworks' in the urban district council office about the lack of drains in Little Poulton Lane. Arguments continued next day in the fish shop on the Breck, owned by one of the councillors. Incandescent with rage a customer, also a councillor, seized a handy cod from the slab and swinging round thumped the shopkeeper with his own fish. Those were the days when serving local government was not just a nice number. It is hoped that the following collection of 250 old photographs will give rise to more chuckles as they remind us of the past.

Catherine Rothwell

1
Poulton-le-Fylde

The Bull Hotel, Market Place, 1892. Before that, in 1880, it was the Black Bull and the landlord was Peter Hornby.

The choir vestry screen in St Chad's Church. This screen was formed from the family pews of the Fleetwood-Heskeths and Rigbys and dates from the seventeenth century. The date 1636 is carved on the door and the initials are those of Alexander Rigby but the rest of the screen, bearing a double-headed eagle, griffin and wheatsheaf, relates to the major county family of the Fleetwood-Heskeths. When Sir Peter Hesketh-Fleetwood was a Member of Parliament an opponent's reply to one of the Baronet's speeches was to pun, 'Sir, you deserve a good threshing', his reference being to the wheatsheaf symbol associated with the family. Both ostentatious pews were removed in 1883 (the Fleetwood-Hesketh version said to resemble a gondola) because they took up far too much room in the church. The plain, beautiful box pews in the north and south gallery are original and have remained untouched since 1751. (*Ron Loomes*)

On the walls of the gallery in St Chad's Church hang the royal arms from 1801 and several diamond-shaped hatchments bearing the arms of various members of the Veale and Fleetwood-Hesketh families. When a person died, usually one of a noble house, a hatchment featuring that person's coat of arms was hung for several months outside their hall or manor house and was eventually moved inside the parish church. These hatchments have all recently been cleaned and layers of varnish removed; the details revealed are of great interest, e.g., griffin, martlets, wolf and wheatsheaf surmounted by 'Blessed are the dead who die in the Lord'. The chancel floor was raised in 1883 at which time the memorial brasses of Geoffrey Hornby and his daughter were placed on the walls. The Hornbys were an influential family in Poulton-le-Fylde. (*Ron Loomes*)

This eighteenth-century font was placed at the foot of the tower of the Parish Church of St Chad's. Found in the garden of the old vicarage, which was demolished in the nineteenth century, it is now closely associated with its original home. Inside the tower are eight bells, but only six are rung. Five were recast between 1741 and 1742 by the famous Ruddle foundry. Another bell (dating from 1865) and two newer ones (1937) came from the Whitechapel foundry. Probably the Ruddle bells were brought by sea to Skippool and then by strong carts to Poulton. The Sundays of October 2001 were strangely silent, the bell clappers having been removed for repair. In 1931 an important find was made in the church tower. A collection of eighty well-wrapped bound volumes presented by Dr Thomas Bray, born in 1721, was uncovered. This may well be the last complete set in such good condition. Dr Bray of the SPCK sent these collections to many parish churches for the clergy's benefit. (*Ron Loomes*)

The east end of St Chad's showing the altar and reredos, the latter erected in memory of Dr W. Riddle, who married the headmistress of Westbourne House School, Miss M. Wilson. The brass chandelier, made by Samuel Smith of Old Bailey, London, is dated 1710. The octagonal Jacobean pulpit on the left has had a chequered career. The carving is similar to the pulpit in Ribchester parish church and so probably dates from about 1636. When a previous pulpit was removed in 1877 the finely carved panels of the present one were discovered and hung on the church walls until 1955 when they were re-assembled. One panel was missing but the carved inscription could be made out as a quotation from Isaiah 58:1: 'Cry aloud, spare not, lift up thy voice like a trumpet'. A semi-circular apse was added by the Revd Thomas Clarke in 1868. The altar rail in this photograph marks the point at which the new apse was built. (*Ron Loomes*)

These arms belong to the Rigby family and are found in the churchyard of St Chad's. The Rigbys used their palatial town house in Poulton in wintertime 'when ways be foul'. Mud and unmade roads made coach travel difficult. Walking was aided by pattens fitted to shoes to raise the wearer out of the mud as there were no pavements. These stone carved arms were originally on the Rigby mansion situated in Market Place. They were preserved when the dwelling was demolished but the date 1693 does not, as has been mistakenly ascribed, relate to the adjacent font, but to the building of the Rigby's town house. (*Ron Loomes*)

The Fleetwood-Hesketh vault, part of St Chad's, where the remains of this important county family lie. Among the coffins and stone sarcophagi is that of Anna Maria, the last of the children of Sir Peter Hesketh's first marriage to die at the age of only eleven. Beneath a glass lid is her embalmed body which was transported from London to Poulton in her pony cart, an event commemorated by her father in a poem. The advowson of St Chad's belonged to the Fleetwoods until after the First World War when it was sold. Sir Peter's brother, the Revd Charles Hesketh, ministered here for a short time. The worn stonework of the vault was skilfully restored by a Southport mason in the 1980s, on the instruction of Colonel Roger Hesketh. (*Ron Loomes*)

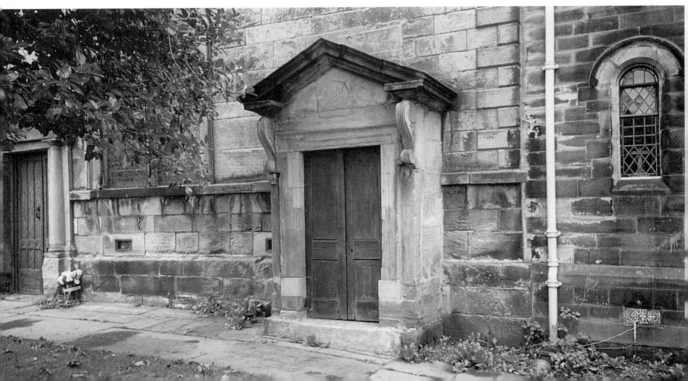

This class of standard VI girls of 1872 could be from any one of the British or National Schools or the High School run by Miss Ellen Aiken and Miss E. Gee in Elletson Street. This photograph may have been discarded prior to residents leaving condemned properties and handing them over to the Drop It demolition firm in the 1960s. Like Autolycus in Shakespeare's *The Winter's Tale*, the 'picker-up of unconsidered trifles', scavengers of what was considered to be rubbish in later years realised they had some valuable reference sources.

Condemned property in Burlington Terrace, *c.* 1957. (*Poulton Library*)

Leckonby House, Great Eccleston, near Poulton, 1860. The original Leckonby House had a stone dated 1754 placed in its gable end by Richard and Mary Leckonby. Mary was the daughter of William Haythornthwaite of Catshaw in Wyresdale and she enjoyed eight years of marriage, her death probably hastened by the squandering habits of her husband who ended up in Lancaster Castle, imprisoned for debt. He never emerged and ill-luck pursued the family. Their only son, William, was killed while hunting in Wyresdale and the first Leckonby House, a magnificent mansion, was burned down in 1766 just four years after Richard had been removed to prison. Portions of the original walls remain and one can still see the gateway through which Richard passed for the last time. He gave orders for the entrance to be bricked up, a final gesture after frittering away a fortune. (*Poulton Library*)

Tourists enjoying, as they still do today, posing in the stocks in Market Place. The locals including the chimney sweep were ready to make a few florins by obliging Poulton's photographer, Mr Lord. James Danson is the name of the black-bearded man with his ventriloquist's dummy, a seafarer naturally! Found in Jennie Danson's collection, this photograph was passed to James's great-granddaughter. James was born in about 1859 and lived in Potts Alley off Market Place.

Beautiful brick-built cottages with stone lintels and windows fitted with glazing bars on the corner of Queen's Square and Chapel Street, *c.* 1860. One of the buildings was an antiques shop in 1959, alongside the Wesleyan chapel, but all the property was razed in the 1960s to make way for new shops. A hairdresser's and a dry cleaner's are now on the site. The even older cottages beyond, rocked with traffic since the introduction of a one-way system, have remained, although one householder was so enraged by the development of the area that he conducted a protest from his roof top. Beyond is Lower Green where May Day revels were once held, to celebrate the fact that the rigours of winter had passed and fresh food was available once more. Home-brewed ale flowed freely and flowers were strewn over the King and Queen of May.

'A friend in need', 1890. More and more postcards were printed for holiday-makers and passing groups brought in by wagonettes touring the Fylde. Being handed a glass of ale was popular, but when the stocks were used in earnest the reality was more likely to be a pelting with rotten eggs and smelly cabbage leaves, part of the prisoner's punishment. Poulton also had a 'cage' where drunken people were locked up for the night to await sentencing later.

Church Street with the lofty, three-storey building known as Twenty Steps, 1883. Along with other old buildings on Ball Street, which completely enclosed the churchyard, this was pulled down in the late nineteenth century. The sign opposite, W. Knight, hung at the Bay Horse Inn, which later became the town hall. Beyond the wall lamp is the Golden Ball Inn. There was a fruit shop, a clogger's, a chip shop and a baker's and confectioner's shop in the street. The large poster on the gable end advertises the 'World Star Turn' showing at the Palace Theatre in Blackpool.

The bells of the Parish Church of St Chad are hung in the great tower, which was built at about the time Charles I was beheaded in 1648. In 1751 the church was taken down to its sandstone base and rebuilt. It was during that time that services were held in the tithe barn and baptisms in the cottages. In the autumn of 2001 the bell clappers required attention and the tower was encased in scaffolding for repairing the stonework. More recently, the church roof has been replaced. Within the massive walled tower are boards dating from the 1930s that are used to record special peals for particular occasions (see below). (*Alison Callum*)

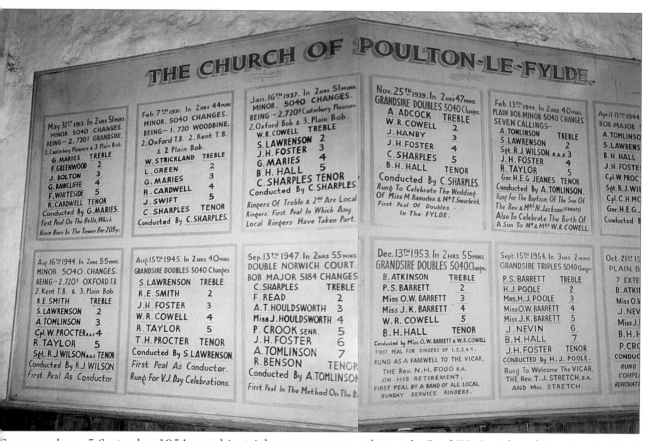

For example on 5 September 1954 grandsire triples were rung to welcome the Revd T.J. Stretch and Mrs Stretch ('Jim' Stretch did sterling work clearing up at Belsen). The first peal of doubles in the Fylde was on 25 November 1939 and there are many records of bell-ringing at births and marriages. Keen photographers regularly trudge up the ancient steps of the church hoping for a fine evening and good views from the top of the tower. (*Alison Callum*)

Poulton band, 1872. The band has flourished for well over a century, taking part in all the main functions of the year – galas, celebrations in the square, carol-singing, parties and, going back to its beginnings, the Club Day processions, events organised by Friendly Societies. Some old inhabitants say it was present and in full blast at the demolition of the mill chimney at the Raby brickworks in 1911. They have practised in many places, including Lloyd's Glassworks on Blackpool Old Road until it was knocked down in the early 1960s. On that occasion some very ancient graves were discovered.

Mr and Mrs Rossall with one of their children, Baden, in front of Staining Windmill, 1884. This windmill differed from other Fylde mills in that it had, at this time, no rear fantail and had to be turned into the wind to set the sails whirling. A wheel, the size of a cartwheel, was fixed outside the top storey and fitted with a rope long enough to reach the ground. This acted as a pulley and turned the windmill top. The sails were sometimes fitted with canvas which could be removed according to the state of the wind. The dusty interior had its walls plastered with broadsheets. Ancient advertisements for dubious remedies vied with playbills announcing visits of the Barnstormers, a group of players, to Poulton's tithe barn (*Marie Marten or Murder in the Red Barn* was a crowd-puller). The weathervane was also unusual in that it was in the shape of a metal fish veering to and fro, its moving parts salvaged from a primitive bicycle. On 22 December 1894, the night that the *Abana* was wrecked in a hurricane, the little fish went wild and the sails of the mill were severely damaged. Joseph Crompton was then the miller. Newspaper headlines read 'Cyclone, 120 mph strikes NW coast of Lancashire'. For the 400 people scattered around the hamlet bordering Poulton-le-Fylde it was certainly a night to remember.

Clarence's Wagonettes outside the Bull Hotel, with its splendid carved wooden inn sign, 1882. In the 1930s the Bull Hotel, facing the stocks in the Square, was where the members of the Pigeon Racing Society met every Friday. The station platform on that day was piled with wicker baskets of competing birds. Each member of the club had a black box containing a clock and simultaneously before the racing all the clocks were synchronised and sealed. Each time a bird returned to its home loft encouraged by maple peas, the ring on its leg was removed, placed in a small metal box and pushed into the clock which recorded the exact time of its insertion. The winner was declared at the next meeting. Breeding and training racing pigeons was costly and painstaking. The birds were exercised via a lad waving a clothes prop to which pennons of coloured cloth were attached. Diet included pellets of Parish's Chemical Food, cod liver oil and meal!

Joseph Cowell, of Higher Green, 1920. Mr Cowell made postal deliveries in Poulton for over fifty years. He retired in 1931. In 1870 the post office was situated in Market Place, facing the stocks, but it moved to Breck Road when Mr Kirkham's house was knocked down. This was not a popular site so the premises moved back to Market Place. When Mrs Wood was post mistress in the 1960s, business was conducted in Church Street and often the post office was crowded to the doors as the population of the town increased quite dramatically. The latest site is a large purpose-built GPO building, part of the Teanlowe Shopping Centre.

The ancient capital of the Fylde would see its importance waning at the time this splendid photograph was taken in 1899. Blackpool's growth and the coming of the railway had made the movement of goods swifter and more efficient. The elegant town houses degenerated into shops and banks and its importance as a port, with the rise of Fleetwood, was no more. In its palmy days the number of inns, fairs and markets conferred status. As a port, it had produced sailcloth. There was a tannery and a skin house at Low Cross, a dye house at the bottom of the Breck and a busy rope works up Sandy Lane but as early as 1846 Poulton's hand-made nails had been replaced by those fashioned by machines. The town still remains an excellent nodal point for commuters to Preston. This view shows the Cyclists' Rest, later demolished, Lawrenson's antique shop, Parkinson's saddler's shop, the Masonic building, the old police station and the medieval cross, stocks and whipping post. The horse-drawn carriage is stopped outside the branch of the Co-operative Society. Next door the newsagent's poster refers to the siege of Ladysmith and the Boer War, which pinpoints the date of the photograph, as does the fact that there is no white area in the centre of the cross's plinth. This was not added until the blackout restrictions of the Second World War were imposed.

Poulton station, 1900. It had been opened in 1896 and was situated at the top of Breck Road, where it had had to be resited following a tragic accident that had occurred at Poulton Curve in 1892. The move from the bottom of Breck Road to the top cost £6,000. In later years, to handle the number of excursion trains passing through Poulton to Blackpool, the number of staff was increased, while the platform was thought to be the longest in the country.

A group of mannequins, mainly drawn from the staff of Windsor Woollies of Poulton-le-Fylde, 1936. The shop's factory was on Station Road. The girls are wearing woollen swimsuits of jacquard weave which were made on looms purchased from Germany and brand-named Windsor Water Woollies. After some altercation about the use of the name Windsor it was eventually accepted by the royal family and the two princesses, Elizabeth and Margaret Rose, wore kilts and jumpers made by the firm. (*Kathleen Brown*)

The Thatched House Tavern, *c.* 1900. The inns of the Fylde, like the windmills, were meeting places for business and pleasure and a cross-section of people are seen here: the innkeeper Nathaniel Charnock with his daughter, railwayman, idle boy, farmer or horse dealer – the horse would have been wearing leather kneecaps, which were sold by saddlers. The man leading it is dressed in a fustian suit and leather leggings. There were a number of inns in the Fylde and Tom Lockwood was innkeeper at the Golden Ball. Transactions were completed in his coffee and newspaper rooms. At the Bull, where rent days were held, Jabez Catterall kept 'the best quality of liquors'. The Green Man, Wheatsheaf, Ship and Sportsman's Arms were all busy on market days. One of the oldest inns in the Fylde was the Guides Inn at Freckleton. In Henry VIII's day guides were appointed by the state to safely convey pilgrims across dangerous sands and fords. The cavernous cellars of the Ship Inn at Freckleton probably hid contraband when John Mayor was landlord, as illegal trafficking and even wrecking went on in the eighteenth century.

The medieval tithe barn, 1903. It was here that corn was threshed and where, before the commutation of tithes, farmers and householders brought a tenth of their assets (corn, lambs, honey, etc.) payable to the lord of the manor, the vicar and other landowners. This snow-covered scene once contributed to Poulton's heart-warming Christmas-card image but sadly the tithe barn was demolished in the early 1960s.

The Prince of Wales's visit to Poulton-le-Fylde, 1927. Poultonians put out numerous flags and leaned from top windows (some even climbed on roof tops) to look down into a crowded Market Place when the Prince of Wales arrived. Mr Baldwin, one of the town's photographers, took this shot. The Prince, later to become the Duke of Windsor, met ex-servicemen after he had opened the Miners' Home at Bispham.

A poster detailing the memorial service held for Queen Victoria in Poulton-le-Fylde, 1901. The service was held at St Chad's, the order of procession being arranged by marshals in Market Place. All those who participated had to wear mourning dress and all window blinds were drawn as the cortège passed along Church Street, Ball Street, Chapel Street, Queen's Square and then back into Market Place before moving on to the church.

Parish of Poulton-le-Fylde

FUNERAL OF HER LATE MAJESTY QUEEN VICTORIA

MEMORIAL SERVICE
AT THE PARISH CHURCH.

It is particularly requested that all persons desirous of joining the Procession to the Parish Church will assemble in the Market Place (East Side), on Saturday Next, at 11-30 o'clock in the Morning.

The Marshals will arrange the Order of the Procession as follows:

Band	Mechanics
Clergy	Order of Buffaloes
Urban District Council	Tontine Society
Freemasons	General Public
Oddfellows	

ROUTE OF PROCESSION:
Market Place, Church Street, Ball Street, Chapel Street, Queen's Square, and Market Place, to the Church.

It is expected that all persons joining the Procession will wear Mourning, and that during the Funeral hours all window blinds be drawn.

Poulton-le-Fylde,
31st January, 1901.

BY ORDER.

An advertisement promoting 'Cadbury's Cocoa for Breakfast', 1910. This drink was destined to make its appearance on the tables of the elegant houses of Breck Road, Lockwood Avenue and Market Place. Census returns show that the 'quality' of Poulton had maids, governesses and even coachmen. In this picture the mistress of the house is seen daintily drawing cocoa from a samovar. The arrival of custard powder, cocoa and tinned goods was welcomed as these early convenience foods made less work.

A rural scene in fields near Tee Woods, 1903. The trees were planted in a T shape and the labourers are from Puddle House Farm, Hardhorn-in-Newton. This was one of the farms owned by James Baines, who set up the three Free Schools in the Fylde at Poulton, Marton and Thornton. The name of this farm possibly derived from the drainage problems with which it was beset, even after valiant attempts had been made to remedy these particular drawbacks. In the 1830s it became notorious for a breed of super rat which proved difficult to exterminate. James purchased the farm from John Pearson and the 'handsome stone' inserted in one of the walls reads, 'This estate given as a perpetual endowment to the Charity School of the Township by Mr James Baines of Poulton who died the 9th day of January 1717 – 22 acres'. Lancashire acres were twice the size of statutory acres.

The demolition of the tall chimney at Raby's Brickcroft, 1911. There was a big turn-out of townspeople to watch the event. Councillor Briggs-Bury lit the fuse and when the dust settled the undamaged bricks were carted off for use elsewhere, bricks being scarce in the Fylde district. The remaining rubble was salvaged by neighbouring residents from Fylde Road and Haworth Crescent for garden retaining walls, and for years later bricks were dug up in allotments nearby. In 1974 the actual brickcroft where the bricks were fired was excavated at 9 Fylde Road, Poulton. When William Ellison was manager in 1889 William Raby was listed as a brick-maker in local trade directories.

Brian and Kathleen M. Haslam alongside the family's new bull-nosed Morris Cowley, 1923. The car cost £300 and was fitted with an electric horn, which was at that time an extra. By 1932 this little girl was also driving, it not being necessary to take a test at that time. The vehicle had its drawbacks, particularly in wet and cold weather in winter despite hot-water bottles, warm clothes and a canvas hood that could be pulled over from the back to the windscreen. The Haslams of Victoria Road (Mr Haslam wrote articles as 'Vortex' for the local newspaper, the *West Lancashire Evening Gazette*) were among the first to have a motor car. They enjoyed picnics after school and travelling on quiet country roads to the beach. On occasions, for example, at the hump-backed bridge at Keppel Lane, Garstang, the children had to get out, place a large stone behind the back wheel and wait until TC 5399 had negotiated the rise. (*Kathleen Brown*)

Market Place, *c.* 1942. At this time traffic was allowed to pass through and on many occasions the famous stocks were damaged. The fish stones and lamp commemorating Queen Victoria's 1887 jubilee and the ancient whipping post can be seen beyond the cross. Richards's well-known ironmonger's shop, the first in the Fylde, was on the far left next to Williams' Café, Mayor's pork butcher's and Mrs Smith's haberdashery shop.

Poulton Gala, 1929. During this period the time-honoured happy procession moved through Market Place but in later years, because of traffic problems, the traditional route was abandoned by order of the council, though locals lamented its passing. The throng in the square, which was bedecked with flags and bunting, cheered the floats of excited children pulled by horses decorated with ribbons and rosettes, their brasses flashing in the sunshine. This procession was on its way to Higher and Lower Green passing through Queen's Square. These were patriotic times and Britannia can be seen in the front cart. The Poulton Morris Dancers were trained by George and Tom Bibby, augmented with troupes from Carleton, Thornton, Fleetwood and Singleton, all of which began dancing in about 1905. Present-day processions wend their way to Cottam Hall Playing Fields at the foot of Rutland Avenue. On one gala day, over twenty years ago, there was so much rain and wind that a marquee was blown down.

The secretarial staff at Windsor Woollies, 1929. Left to right: Hilda Ross, who was in charge and a fully trained secretary from Manchester, Mary Bradbury and Miss C. Whalley, whose father was headmaster of Thornton Free School. (*Kathleen Brown*)

The Windsor Woollies Christmas party at Jenkinson's Café, Blackpool, 1930. Among the numerous staff of the Windsor Woollies Castle Works factory (a real family firm started in 1907) were Mr and Mrs Benjamin Windsor, William Windsor, Albert V. Windsor, Alys Milner (chief model), Peggy Fitzgerald, Phyllis Swales, Mary Bradbury, Bertha Simmons, Mr Rains (traveller) and the youngest member of the Windsor family, Neville, aged three, all of whom are seen here. Neville was also used as a model. Benjamin, the founder, was born in 1872. (*Kathleen Brown*)

Cover of the programme of *The Rising Generation*, 1925. This was the first production to be staged in the new St Chad's Church hall in Vicarage Road on Friday and Saturday, 11 and 12 December 1925. It was presented by Poulton-le-Fylde Amateur Operatic and Dramatic Society and produced by Jack Kemp. In the programme the play is described as 'a new comedy in three acts by Wyn Weaver and Laura Leycester'. During the performance the Blackpool Amateur Symphony Orchestra, conducted by Percy M. Dayman, played selections.

Poulton-le-Fylde
Amateur Operatic and
Dramatic Society

present

The

Rising Generation

St. Chad's Church Hall,

Friday   -   December 11th, 1925.
Saturday - December 12th, 1925.

A scene from *The Rising Generation*, 1925. (*William Yates*)

Fyldean hockey team, who also played at Moorland Road, 1920. (*Sheila Isherwood*)

Opposite, above: Miss Simmons's class at Westbourne House School, Lockwood Avenue, 1926. Back row, left to right: Irene Foster, Hilda Pye, Barbara Winder, Kathleen Buckley, Rene Gornall, Joan Staskia, Vera Leigh, Vera Davies, -?-. Seated: Hilda Starr, Kathleen Haslam, Eileen Laurie, Miss Simmons, Vera Thomas, Mary Starr, Joan Evans. This private school produced good scholars who went on to pursue useful and productive careers. A school ahead of its time, there was a purpose-built gymnasium and drama, music and dancing were offered in addition to the normal curriculum. Belle Chrystal, a pupil in the 1930s, became a well-known actress on BBC Radio. She cycled daily to Westbourne House from her home at Rossall Grange Farm. (*Kathleen Brown*)

Opposite, below: The Fyldean Cricket Club, 1920. This was the name that the club was known by in the 1920s. They held fixtures in Thornton, Bispham, Poulton and frequently played at Whittingham Hospital. Their headquarters were on Moorland Road, Poulton-le-Fylde, as they are today. Back row, left to right: ? Fairbrother, Eric Robinson, -?-, Ronnie Fairbrother, -?-, -?-. Seated: -?-, -?-, -?-, J. Hopkinson, T. Edge, Noel Shaw. (*Sheila Isherwood*)

The wheelwright Mr J.R. Wainman (left) outside Staining Smithy, *c.* 1880. The other gentleman could be John Riding or Richard Blacoe, who were blacksmiths at Staining at this time. Within a relatively confined area encompassing Staining, Carleton, Great Singleton, Bispham, Poulton and Thornton the 1882 directory lists eight blacksmiths, with two being situated on Station Road in Poulton a few years later. Blacksmithing and whitesmithing ran in families and the Simmons and the Swarbricks were well known for these trades in late-nineteenth-century Fylde. The same might be said of boot- and shoe-makers, the Sandhams and the Cleggs being foremost in this field. (*Norman Short*)

The Mary Macarthur Home on Breck Road, 1930. It was built when convalescent homes were needed in the early twentieth century. In the 1980s it became a home for the elderly. The Joseph Cross Memorial Convalescent Home, also on Breck Road, was built in 1933. Those who worked in the cotton industry came here to recuperate, hailing from all over Lancashire. This was converted to the new Wyre Civic Centre and re-opened on 4 January 1988.

William Yates (right) of Poulton-le-Fylde with his Danish friend Walt Rosenberg, 1935. One of a party of Baines Grammar School boys, William travelled to Denmark on a return visit the following year. The boys were glad to see Elsinore as they were studying Shakespeare's play *Hamlet* at the time. (*William Yates*)

A sixty-one key Verbreeck musical organ parked at the top of Hardhorn Road leading into Queen's Square, Poulton, during the town's Victorian weekend in 1986. The organ belongs to Peter and Judy Wareing of Wrea Green, near Poulton, and features moving figures. After Poulton it visited Lytham and spent a sunny Saturday enlivening the scene to raise money for Cancer Research. With this same purpose, it has since been brought to Blackpool and other Fylde towns. (*William Yates*)

This falconer passed through Poulton-le-Fylde in the summer of 1970, camping behind the Thatched House Tavern in Ball Street. He provided entertainment for residents and visitors to the Victorian market. The bird on his arm was said to be a red kite. (*William Yates*)

This 'Happy Xmas' photographic memento features young Bill Yates at Garstang Road East. Bill narrowly missed going down with HMS *Hood* in May 1941 when many lives were lost. Bill and twelve other sailors were saved by being transferred to shore for a special training course at the last moment. Bill eventually took up teaching as a career and became deputy headmaster of Highfield School. Like his son, he showed early promise as a musician. (*William Yates*)

a Happy Xmas

A group of boys and staff outside Baines Grammar School, 1935. They are possibly gathered as part of celebrations for the silver jubilee of King George V and Queen Mary. The school is thought to have had its origins in 1717, as did Marton and Thornton schools, all endowed by James Baines who lived in a house facing the stocks in Market Place, later tenanted by Stephen Burridge, customs officer for the port of Poulton. (*William Yates*)

Baines Grammar School, *c.* 1900. The gable end reads 'Baines's Grammar School founded by James Baines A.D. 1717', and this was a feature of the original building as described by member of staff, Mr Pagett, in his history of the school. (*William Yates*)

Kathleen Haslam leads the prize bullock, Mr A. Lowe's champion from Out Rawcliffe, at the Poulton Christmas Fat Stock Show, 1931. Other winners were Mr T. Barlow of Carleton and Mr J.R. Lawson of Weeton with his pair of turkey cockerels. Regular sales of livestock were held at the Poulton-le-Fylde Auction Mart Company Ltd, 9 Tithebarn Street. They were organised by Heywood R. Tracey, agricultural auctioneer and valuer. In those days a special slade had to be constructed at Poulton station as the numbers of livestock being transported increased. It also became obvious that auctions needed to be moved from Market Place. Pens were set up behind the Golden Ball Inn and business transacted away from the main shopping area. This was to the relief of residents because frisky heifers had been known to wander freely and create minor havoc. (*Kathleen Brown*)

Agnes Stirzaker in the cobbled farmyard at Stirzaker's Farm, Skippool, Poulton-le-Fylde, with mare and foal, *c.* 1936. Cobbles were brought from the seashore and were widely used as excellent, hard-wearing (if uncomfortable to the feet) building materials. Over a hundred years ago Market Place was covered with these cobbles which were referred to by the locals as 'petrified kidneys'. (*Robert Gibson*)

The WVS All Services Canteen, which operated in Poulton during the Second World War. This organisation finally moved to Weeton but a substitute canteen was set up behind the post office in Market Square (which was then near the Stocks Café) in what had been the hockey club pavilion. (*Kathleen Brown*)

Mrs N. Haslam crowning the Poulton Festival Queen on fields behind the 'New Road' (Garstang Road West), *c.* 1928. One of the first houses to be built on the road was named Kinders and it was also the first to have an electricity supply, which was generated in the garage and set up by Poulton electrician Mr Buckley. (*Kathleen Brown*)

Hutton Grammar School's rugby football team, 1942/43. The rugby and cricket teams played fixtures against Baines Grammar School. This was a time when these seventeen and eighteen year olds were apprehensively contemplating joining up for the Second World War. Second from the left on the back row is Rae Hammond, who later joined the Foreign Service in Nigeria and on his return to Britain, when Nigeria gained independence in 1960, became manager of the Everyman Theatre in Cheltenham. In the centre wearing the cap, captain of rugby, was C.J. Woodcock who became headmaster of Highfield School, Blackpool, many years later.

Grange Park School, near Poulton's boundary, produced a well-costumed nativity play at Christmas 1953. Kneeling at the front of the stage is Peter Yates who in later years became a professional actor and musician. He provided music at each performance of a play based on the works of Catherine Cookson, which ran for many months and toured the north-west. He was a gifted entertainer who played the piano, violin, hurdy-gurdy and sitar, and he loved to turn his talent to any unusual instrument. (*William Yates*)

Dudley Hall, 1953. This thatched cottage in Blackpool Old Road was one of the last to go when demolition of old property was ordered by the council. The tenant held out for a long time but eventually this most interesting property was razed. It stood on the site where Poulton Library was built. The cottage's name is linked with those of Empsom and Dudley. In Henry VIII's reign Richard Empsom was made Chancellor of the Duchy of Lancaster and with Dudley, who was also a lawyer, the pair worked as the King's debt collectors and imposed cruel sanctions. It is said that they operated from this cottage when they visited Poulton in 1505, which suggests that the property was very old indeed. In the area of Poulton, Thornton and Bispham, cottages were often named halls, for example, Cockle Hall at Stanah and Fanny Hall on the cliffs at Bispham. The last-named eventually fell into the sea.

A Preston & Wyre Railway marker, 1953. This stone was one of only three remaining markers that were used to track the railway line from Preston to Fleetwood. These markers were set up in the 1830s, when the railway was under construction, ready for opening in 1840. This stone was in a garden at the bottom of Lockwood Avenue, Poulton. Another, on the avenue itself and opposite Westbourne House (now council offices), disappeared when the road was resurfaced in the 1970s.

A celebration in the church hall, Poulton-le-Fylde, 1959. The Revd N.H. Fogg, Curate and Bishop Anthony Hoskyns Abrahall are seen in the centre of the group. Two splendid cakes are asking to be cut and there is a lovely display of flowers in a silver holder – whatever was the occasion? This is obviously the top table with other tables forking off – could it be an event to celebrate the first fifty years of the Mothers' Union? (*Robert Gibson*)

A group of finely dressed people, 1950. Back row, left to right: Mr Jolly, Jenny Hesketh, Doris ?, -?-, Mrs Walne, Mrs Spencer, Mr Spencer, Mr Walne. Front row: Mrs Jolly, Edna ?, Elizabeth ?. Jenny Hesketh was very fond of Alsatian dogs, never having less than two. Each year she went to Crufts in London. She led a busy social life in Poulton besides her book-keeping at Skippool Farm. (*Robert Gibson*)

Looking across the River Wyre towards the River House Restaurant at Skippool Creek, 1957. 'This is my favourite walk' writes the sender of this postcard. 'We have just had coffee under the tree.' Skippool was the place on the pool where the River Skipton entered, draining from Marton Mere. The Celtic word 'pyll' means pool or creek and can be seen in the name Pilling. Pool was once a common word in the district denoting a small port; for example, 'Poolton' means the town on the pool. Close by Skippool Creek lay the toll bridge at Shard (now gone) and Wardleys Creek, which was a busy place in the mid-nineteenth century with as many as seven ships being known to arrive at the same time. William Swarbrick ferried passengers between Cockle Hall and Wardleys for fifty years. He remembered cotton and flax being delivered and stored in the warehouse. Before Fleetwood was constructed, the firms of Swainson's and Birley's had quays built. The Wardleys Hotel was originally called the Royal Oak and had hoists fitted for unloading cargoes. A cottage was used as the customs house and when trade slackened ships brought guano to fertilise the drained marshlands of the Fylde.

Millstones from the four-storey corn mill that once stood in Chapel Street and belonged to Mr Parkinson, 1960. These millstones were rescued by Mr Walter Heapey, who worked hard to preserve Marsh Mill from dereliction. Mr Heapey arranged for these stones to be placed in front of Marsh Mill but in the making of the multi-million-pound complex sited around Marsh Mill, which is now the only working windmill in what was once 'Windmill Land', these interesting items have been moved. (*Norman Short*)

This plumed two-cornered black hat is the High Sheriff's hat and was worn by Peter Hesketh in a mile-long procession from Poulton to Lancaster in 1833. Peter, who became Sir Peter Hesketh-Fleetwood, was lord of the manor and the founder of Fleetwood as a port and watering place. The occasion of his journey was the customary triumphal meeting up with the judges at Lancaster Assizes. They were escorted to the Judge's Lodgings and trials of criminals were conducted the next day after a great feast. The sessions that followed frequently involved hangings for minor offences, for example, John Battersby was sentenced to 'transportation for 7 years for stealing a pair of shoes from Richard Warbrick' by Sir John Gerrard, who was High Sheriff before Peter. At his procession Peter rode a 'white' horse and had given instructions to search the county for grey horses to pull the coaches.

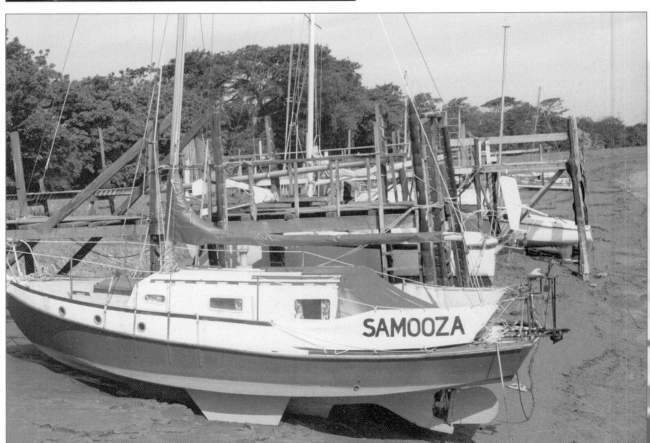

The *Samooza* among boats moored at Skippool Creek, 1962. Poulton was originally a 'pool village' like others in the Fylde. In 1825 warehouses were built at Skippool and Wardleys Creek by the Blackburn brothers of Thistleton village. They made a fortune from this, much of which William spent on estates in the Fylde. Flax for Birley's Mill at Kirkham was unloaded at Wardleys. The Birley company had a contract with the British government to make soldiers' uniforms.

Catherine Rothwell, librarian, local historian and author, by the preaching cross in the churchyard of St Chad's, spring 1972. The steps of the preaching cross, which once was sited on the boundary of the village, are original and very old. The shaft of the cross had to be replaced. It once served as a sundial, though this was not its original purpose, but in the curacy of the Revd Mr Bulpit the gnomon was stolen. Now part of the garden of remembrance, where ashes are interred, it is usually piled with fresh flowers. The cross served as a halt when corpses had to be carried a long way for burial in Poulton churchyard. The steps also afforded an opportunity to take refreshment and offer prayers for the dead. Mourners came from as far away as Marton. Nowadays the glorious sight of snowdrops and crocuses draws larger crowds each spring.

The *Flying Scotsman* steams past Poulton-le-Fylde signal-box in the days when it was owned by Alan Pegler, 1970. To great local excitement Mr Pegler was on the footplate with an experienced engine driver beside him and they smiled and chatted to railway enthusiasts crowding the station platform. It was a magnificent sight to witness this green giant approaching and gently moving off again on its journey to Blackpool. Not long after this momentous occasion the *Flying Scotsman* was shipped across to the USA as an attraction. Another great day for 'gricers' was the passing through Poulton of the locomotive *Mallard*.

Butler's Farm, 1969. Butler's Farm, the whole remaining area of which became the Teanlowe Shopping Centre, relinquished many of its fields for house-building in the 1960s. This rural scene is now the busy heart of Poulton. The tall building was the slaughter house, which belonged to Mr Arthur Butler, and was demolished in the mid-1960s along with many very old and derelict cottages and two Georgian houses on Tithebarn Street, which was once known as 'Doctors Row'.

Rutland Avenue, one of the new housing areas, along with Chester, Ryland and Rydal Avenues, which was built on Butler's farm land, 1969. The car is a top-of-the-range Morris Oxford with leather upholstery. Behind Rutland Avenue, doctors' premises and sheltered accommodation were established. In the early years animals from what remained of the farm were apt to come through chestnut palings and wander on unmade Rutland Avenue and what became Queensway.

The mayoral party on Remembrance Sunday 1974. Councillor and Mrs MacGregor were the first mayor and mayoress of the newly formed Borough of Wyre, so the mayoral car's registration number was WBC 74 (Wyre Borough Council). Next to Councillor MacGregor is Leslie Dickinson, deputy mace-bearer, and at the far end Alderman Funk. Poulton, Thornton-Cleveleys and Garstang became part of the Borough of Wyre but other sections of the old Fylde merged into the Borough of Fylde. (*Ann and Leslie Dickinson*)

Bill Scott, 1981. Bill is an internationally renowned chef whose patrons have included politician Ted Heath. He runs his well-known restaurant from the River House on the banks of the River Wyre at Skippool. Originally a yeoman farmer's dwelling, the house was built in 1836. In the sixteenth and seventeenth centuries Russian ships sailed up the River Wyre to the ports of Skippool and Wardleys, bringing grain, cotton and flax. Even slave ships arrived from the West Indies. The emigrant ship *The Six Sisters* (named after the Swarbrick girls of Skippool) sailed to America from here and this is where the barque *Hope* was built, ill-fated in spite of its name. The area is now a modern marina, the old warehouses all demolished, but the fame of the River House, run by Bill Scott and by his mother Jean Scott before him, has spread throughout the country and abroad. Hotpot and poached scallops (caught off the Isle of Man) are his specialities.

Eddie and Catherine Rothwell of Poulton ran a stall at the charity market held at St John's Church just before Christmas 1988. There were many stalls and Eddie and Catherine's was to raise funds for the Tinnitus Society. Items on the stall were made and donated by members from Poulton, Thornton, Bispham and even as far afield as Morecambe. A total of £200 was raised.

The path through Poulton churchyard leading to Chapel Street, 1962. The graveyard was closed for burial in 1883 and there was further change in 1868 when the apse was built. This path consists mainly of huge slabs detailing deaths from the eighteenth and nineteenth centuries. Before the levelling of the churchyard in 1972 an index of all the gravestones was made and placed in Poulton Library for posterity.

Mains Hall, 1963. Situated between Singleton and Poulton, Mains Hall is now a country house restaurant but has an interesting history. Most of the hall was built between 1600 and 1700, the Hesketh family having acquired the estate from the widowed Countess of Derby. Built as three sides of a quadrangle, the open end faced away from the River Wyre. There are still traces of a moat. The river's proximity may well have aided smugglers evading the customs officers. Silks and spirits, under cover of darkness, slipped past or into the hall and Roman Catholic priests could also steal away and take a boat up river. There is a priest hole concealed in the hall. The Heskeths would not accept the new religion and mass was held in the private chapel in secret. Mains Hall was frequently a hiding place for Cardinal William Allen (right), born at Rossall Hall, when he made trips from the continent during Elizabeth I's reign. Another royal connection was with the Prince of Wales, later George IV, in 1785. Maria Anne Fitzherbert may have met the Prince at Mains Hall. She was a Roman Catholic but an Anglican clergyman conducted their secret marriage service. A Royal scandal ensued. Mrs Fitzherbert's boudoir at Mains Hall, for she was a regular visitor there, may still be pointed out. She enjoyed an allowance of £6,000 a year and died at Brighton in 1837.

GUILIELMUS ALANUS, S.R.E. CARDINALIS, S.T.T. Duac. Archiepus Mechlin. designatus, obiit Romæ Aᵒ MDXCIV.

The last passenger train leaves Wyre Dock station to travel through Thornton, Poulton and on to Preston, the old Preston & Wyre Railway route, 1970. In the 1930s Poulton station was well staffed. The waiting room in winter had a comforting fire to welcome passengers, horse-hair-covered benches and a W.H. Smith's magazine and newspaper stall. Of the many porters, one operated a goods lift by ropes. Perambulators could be lowered to the platforms and placed in the luggage van, along with cycles, fish and pigeons! A special platform, fitted with a ramp and leading on to the Breck, was for cattle arriving for the auction mart conducted twice weekly. When Poulton ran its own agricultural show the volume of livestock traffic increased enormously. Jack Roskell, whose father had a small farm at Poulton Curve halt, issued tickets from the booking office. In the early 1930s the return fare from Poulton to Blackpool was 3*d* and a monthly contract 7*s* 6*d*.

This collection of buildings was part of Butler's Farm behind Long's bookshop and what was then the town hall and are seen here in 1964. They include the lock-up used by the village policeman and the beadle before him in the eighteenth and nineteenth centuries. It is not known when the stocks were last used for punishment but it may have been in the mid-1770s. The tiny lock-up was a dark, noisome place, windowless and with little room to move. Prisoners would be confined there awaiting judgement from the court house, which was situated in Queen's Square at the top of Hardhorn Road, originally Sheaf Street.

The late Bill Hailstones, who sang with the Festival Jazzmen, performing at the social club in Hardhorn Road, 1973. Bill, a saxophonist, became crippled with arthritis in the 1950s and could no longer play an instrument but he had a fine singing voice. A frequent request was for Bill to render 'Old Rocking Chair'. (*The Festival Jazzmen*)

The Festival Jazzmen welcoming the *Orient Express* to the Fylde, 1980. From left to right: Bill Hailstones (seated), Ron Strachan (seated with banjo), -?-, Tony Tolley, Derek Johnson, Cyril Wroe, Cyril Robinson. This popular group, which started in 1974 at the Queen's Hotel, Lower Green, has played venues all over the Fylde during the past two decades. Familiar figures at all Fylde village fête days, they have been sponsored by the *West Lancashire Gazette*. They serenaded a restored vintage American Buick motor car which was donated by Mr Don Sidebottom to the fine collection of vintage models at Holker Hall. Fleetwood Freeport, the marina built on the former docks that attracts people from all over the country, have had their visitors enlivened by this dynamic group. There have been great musical occasions when first-class performers such as Digby Fairweather and Ray Williams have joined the group and these have attracted jazz enthusiasts from other parts of Lancashire. (*The Festival Jazzmen*)

2

Thornton-le-Fylde

The children of Baines Endowed School, Thornton, 1926. (*Joan Currie*)

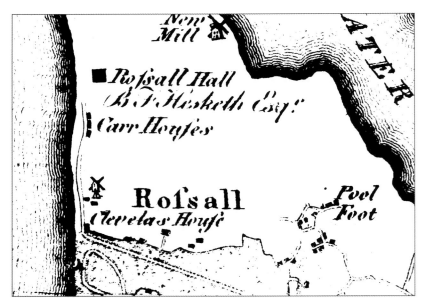

A detail from Yates's map of 1786. This section shows the site of Rossall windmill on the seashore and Cleveleys House (Clevelas Houfe) with the track running towards Rossall Hall where Bold Fleetwood Hesketh then lived. The track and windmill were eventually washed away as the ever-encroaching sea eroded the coast. Over the centuries 3 miles of land have been lost. (*Lancashire Record Office*)

Marsh Mill, Thornton, *c.* 1902. This mill was built by Ralph Slater, millwright, in 1794 for Bold Fleetwood Hesketh, uncle of Peter Hesketh, the founder of Fleetwood. Bold insisted that all his tenants should have their corn ground at his mill. Ralph Slater also built the windmills at Pilling and Clifton in the Fylde but Thornton's has a varied history and its sails can still turn to this day. For generations it ground different grades of flour but when white flour was mainly in demand at the beginning of the twentieth century, the windmill was unable to produce it and factories took over. Thornton Mill ground coarse meal for farm use until 1922, Mr Tomlinson being the last miller. In the 1930s it was used as a café but later it was the scene of a tragic accident when two ladies who hoped to purchase it came to have a look round. They stepped on to the platform at the top and it gave way killing one of them. Thornton Urban District Council eventually bought the windmill and restoration work was ongoing under the guidance of Mr Walter Heapey. It remains a striking symbol of the ancient Amounderness region of Lancashire. (*Charles Ashton*)

The Landmark, one of the many drawings by Sea Dog (the late J.C. Houghton), a regular visitor to the Fylde coast since 1921. Long before the coastal towns appeared, this conical heavy wooden structure like a primitive 'Jungle Jim' climbing frame was sited in a field at Rossall Grange Farm. It was probably in 1740 that the Lancaster Commissioners placed it to guide ships heading for Lancaster Port and Glasson Dock. More than one landmark was washed away for Rossall Point was wild and stormy. The name Old Angersholme (now Anchorsholme) reflects the sea's mood. In 1861 the Revd St Vincent Beechey, walking with the mathematics master from Rossall School, saw one landmark topple, undermined by heavy waves. A metal cage was fixed to the top of the structure, but it was never illuminated. It was intended that a warning fire be lit inside the cage in times of emergency, such as invasion. Somewhere deep in the sands this cage lies buried. Preserved by thick coats of tar, the landmark was no longer needed once Fleetwood acquired its lighthouses and in the late 1920s it was pulled down and carted off for firewood.

Sea Dog, 1937. John Charles Houghton, artist and musician, sketching and painting in Bowland.

The staff of the *Fleetwood Chronicle*, which covered news from Fleetwood, Thornton, Bispham and north of the sands, 1866. The paper was started by William Porter on 11 November 1843 and sold for 3*d*. The first newspaper in the Fylde, it was printed on a hand press in a room above a stable. The little boy seen here is holding up a page announcing the death of Sir Peter Hesketh Fleetwood, lord of the manor and one-time owner of the great tithes of Thornton. All Improvement Commissioners' meetings, tide tables and shipping information were reported in the paper and it is obvious that the prevailing problem along the coastal strip was blowing sand. Most of the Improvement Commissioners' meetings bring up the subject and under the 1842 Improvement Act, which was far-sighted in its recommendations (for example, no polluting of streams, no firing of chimneys, cesspools to be covered, no buildings in future to be thatched), they were hampered only by lack of funds.

The *Ben My Chree II* (known as the '*Ben Machree*') leaving the Fylde coast, bound for the Isle of Man, 1879. Built in 1875, this photograph was taken before she was 'boilered' and had four funnels. Steamer service to the island and to Belfast had commenced on 7 October 1841, advertised as offering the 'Best route to Belfast and Londonderry: The North Lancashire Steam Navigation Company's iron steamers Prince of Wales and Princess Alice. For Londonderry, the powerful steamer Robert Napier'. It was great fun watching sea-going vessels off Bispham, Norbreck and Thornton-Cleveleys.

Sea and river fishing have long involved mariners and countrymen along the Fylde coast and inland so this 'Fisherman's Prayer' is apt. The sender of the postcard has written on the back, 'May your lines run freely and never touch rock bottom – the fish dish was delish!' (*Ann and Leslie Dickinson*)

Cleveleys, 1890. Visitors had been encouraged to visit here ever since May 1785 when John Salthouse placed an advertisement in the *Manchester Mercury* for his inn or bathing house which he had 'genteely fitted up'. The early boarding houses were close to the sea with only sand, marram grass and a primitive fence for protection.

Councillors returning to the council offices after the church service on Civic Sunday, 1929. Thornton became a separate parish in 1868 and Cleveleys was created a separate parish in 1911. The first parish council was elected on 4 December 1894 and had seven members: Robert Tyler, John Bradshaw, Christopher Riley, William Walsh, Thomas Walsh, Seth Bond, William Betney. Their powers were limited but by May 1927, when the districts were joined and called Thornton-Cleveleys Urban District, the souvenir town guide described the area as 'a garden resort and a children's paradise'. On the right is Swarbrick's Pointer Farm which was later demolished and a bank built on the site. Beyond, on the other corner of Victoria Road East, is Dr Rhodes's house.

Mary Elizabeth Hopkinson, 1888. At this time she lived at Booth Farm, Tottington, Bury, but the family later moved to Thornton-le-Fylde, where there were twenty-three farms recorded in Slater's Directory of 1882. (*Sheila Isherwood*)

John and Annie Louisa Ashton (born in 1865) and part of their family, 1892. The children are, from left to right: Scott (born 1894), Charles (born 1892) and Grace (born 1893). In later years Scott produced a book about the history of the Parish Church of St Chad. Annie Louisa died at the age of eighty-four and was buried at Thornton parish church. Very little of the area was built up in those early days – Hawthorne Road and others were filled with picturesque Fylde cottages covered with thatch which in later years was replaced by corrugated metal. As tiles and slates became common roofing materials, the art of thatching began to die out and Willow Cottage and Poolfoot Cottage were the last to remain. Parr's Cottage in Meadows Avenue was once a showpiece with its spinning wheel, eighteenth-century oak chests, thatched porch, gardens and hedges. Before the making of the sea wall, high tides used to reach as far inland as Parr's Cottage. (*Charles Ashton*)

T. Kirkham's blacksmith's shop in the shadow of Marsh Mill where horses were brought via Atkinson's field, 1890. Jack Breckell's wheelwright's shop was also in the mill yard, blacksmith's being necessary to heat the circular metal that bound farm cart wheels. At 110 ft high with six storeys, Marsh Mill towered over neighbouring buildings, and was 102 ft in circumference at the base. The four wooden sails were each 35 ft long. In July 1979 a new oak beam on which the sails rested was hoisted into place.

Children at Thornton Church Road School, 1895. The third boy on the second row from the back, with his arms folded, is the son of John Parr of Parr's Cottage. Mr Hardman, left, stands sternly holding his 'parchment' to show he is qualified to teach a class of forty-two or more. The young lady 'pupil teacher' was in charge of the children on the front row. Starched white pinafores, clogs, gold watch guards and 'leg o' mutton' sleeves were clearly in fashion. (*Charles Ashton*)

A class from Carleton C. of E. School with their headmaster, Mr Wrightson, July 1958. Back row, left to right: Eric Knott, Stuart Duckett, Michael Marriott, Malcolm Woof, Robert Laing, Frank Worthing, John Gilliam, Malcolm Parker. Among the girls in this photograph are Susan Hudson, Lynne Bates and Jean Scupholme. Carleton was part of Thornton and Fleetwood School Board, which was formed in 1878, although by 1885 the two main districts had separated in terms of educational provision. Minute books commenced on 10 January 1878 when only one Thornton man, Robert Tyler, yeoman farmer, was on the committee. In that year there were 317 children up to the age of 13 living in Thornton. Mr Tyler and Captain Martin, mariner, set out purchasing land between Thornton church and Fisher's Fold. Mrs Warbreck sold them a plot for £260 and the building of a school was begun. The master of the New Board School at Thornton had to be married and his wife able to teach sewing. There were thirty-six applicants for the post of headmaster. Mr J.M. Carter from Nottingham was appointed on a salary of £75 per year. The cleaner, Mrs Cowell, was paid 1s 6d a week and within two years Mrs Annie Carter, wife of the headmaster, was accepted as assistant at £20 per annum. At that time there were more than eighty pupils at the school. (*Joan Currie*)

Mr and Mrs Freeborn and their family outside Marsh Mill, 1897. Edmund Freeborn was appointed manager in 1896, helped by his sons Robert and William. They chained the sacks together on the bottom floor and hauled them through trap doors to the top of the mill, the dust floor, where Mr Freeborn unchained them and set about the milling. For Queen Victoria's jubilee in June 1887, Marsh Mill was whitewashed and the sails and fantail painted. The Freeborns were a family of ten who lived in the house in the mill grounds, growing their own fruit and vegetables, which was the responsibility of the older girls.

John Ashton, c. 1880. In the 1880s John acquired a penny-farthing and cycled regularly until the age of eighty. As a child he attended school half-time, working on a local farm in the afternoons. Helping out at Thornton post office he would walk all the way to Singleton to deliver parcels. If snow fell, he and his brother Richard followed and counted the telegraph poles. At the age of nineteen he set up a shoe-making and repairing shop in the village until he himself took over the post office. Telegrams were sent by Wheatstone's mechanical transmitter on a direct line to Fleetwood and should a villager need a postal order, the money was handed over to John who purchased the orders in Preston. In the new premises at Thornton John acquired the first telephone in the village. A pig was kept ready for slaughter in the autumn and a cow produced the milk for John's family of nine, so they were almost self-supporting. (*Charles Ashton*)

The Pendlebury family on the sands at Thornton, 1905. This postcard was written to Mrs Nelson at Hastings Road (no house number was considered necessary) and is most correctly addressed to Thornton-le-Fylde. (*Sheila Isherwood*)

Mrs Alice Ann Scholes, 1926. Born in Thornton as Alice Moorcroft, she was a well-known figure in the area. She was the first to settle in Stockdove Way after the Cleveleys Cottage Exhibition, which ran for three months and was held at the entrance to West Drive in 1906. A large brochure invited builders and architects to submit plans for reasonably priced homes with three bedrooms, a bathroom, a garden, mains water and sewerage and gas and electricity supplies. This was, at the time, a revolutionary concept and it attracted the attention of such eminent figures as Sir Edwin Lutyens. There were prizes of £150 awarded for the best architectural designs and plans, and these were won by local builders Albert Dove and Bertram Drummond respectively. All detached and semi-detached property sold quickly. Mrs Scholes made a wise purchase. (*Sheila Isherwood*)

Thornton Gala, 1912. These people are travelling past the new premises of the post office and Marsh Mill. As at Carleton and Poulton, the whole township participated which explains the presence of so many ladies in ankle-length dresses and floral hats. The horses pulling the carts and landaus were well groomed, their polished brasses shining like gold alongside coloured rosettes and ribbons. The children must have been very well behaved in such crowded carts, as there were no accidents reported at these long-anticipated gatherings. It was 'Joy Day' in Thornton, as the gala used to be described. It began as Club Day over 100 years ago, when the Mechanics Friendly Society tramped around the district with silk banners. It was less of a carnival then and the event ended with a service at Thornton parish church. However, as the day's popularity grew, sports and the crowning of the rose queen were added to the list of activities. (*Charles Ashton*)

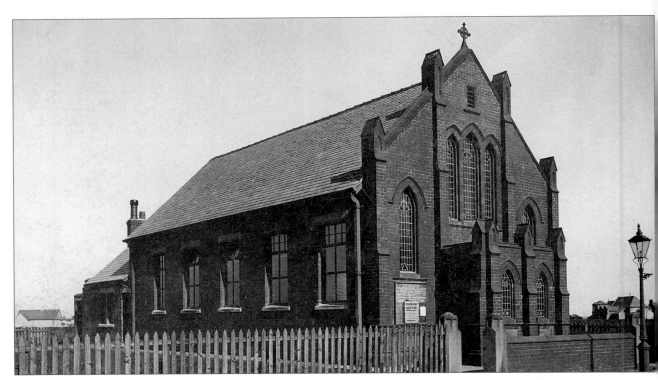

'Happy Harry' showing off his bicycle, 1905. He cycled all the way to Baines Grammar School from Hambleton and visited his friends in Thornton. Cycling on the flat Fylde terrain with no motor traffic around was a great way of getting about and keeping fit. On the back of this card Harry has written, 'I hope you are cheerful'. (*Charles Ashton*)

The Ashton family on holiday on the Isle of Man, 1900s. The horse-drawn Victoria was very useful especially for holidays when visitors were taken to see the sights. John Ashton is at the front, nearest the camera. (*Charles Ashton*)

Opposite, below: The Congregational church in Kensington Road off Beach Road, 1912. In 1901 when Cleveleys was a small seaside community of thatched cottages and farms, villagers made their way to the original Beach Road Congregational church by the light of storm lanterns or candles in glass jars. In winter, when tides were high and winds roared there were complaints that the congregation could not hear the sermon! That first building became a garage and for years the text 'Oh worship the Lord in the beauty of holiness' was to be seen on the wall above where the altar had stood. The church seen here was in use in 1912 but has since been replaced. Cleveleys Avenue was a cinder path through fields and Rossall Road a narrow country lane bordered with hawthorn bushes. The rural nature of this district remained for years, although an ever-increasing population gradually changed the 'garden village' into a bustling town of bricks and mortar. In 1906 visitors and residents alike to the Ye Tea House could buy a 9*d* pot of tea with bread and butter and strawberries and cream. A meat tea cost 1*s*. (*Mr W. Leadbetter*)

Class 1, Burn Naze School, 1921. The children have obviously all obeyed the instruction to fold their arms. In those days strict discipline was maintained and the three Rs drilled into young heads by rote, which meant constantly chanting the same thing over and over again until it was memorised. (*Joan Currie*)

Thornton village, 1906. Seen here are the miller's cottages and the drying kiln, which were later demolished although Marsh Mill itself still stands today, part of a multi-million-pound complex opened by the Duke of Westminster on 2 May 1990. On the left is Church Road and on the right the Gardener's Arms Inn, hidden by trees. Gardner, a family name, became Gardener when a new inn was built.

A row of terraced cottages in the centre of Thornton, 1913. Tenants of these cottages, near the Gardener's Arms, whitewashed the pebbled garden walls thickly to hold the ageing structures together but also, as with back-yard walls and privies, to keep them clean. Childhood ailments such as measles and scarlet fever were often fatal. Winter and summer, children were 'well wrapped up' to prevent them catching cold. To modern eyes the results are over-dressed and fussy, but not without charm, as in this photograph. (*Charles Ashton*)

This group may well have been participating in the 1927 Thornton Gala, which was particularly ambitious with the procession said to be over a mile long. The people and their decorated bicycles (a feature of Bispham's galas) include Herbert Ashton at the front in a straw boater. The second bike from the left belonged to Joe Graham, who worked on the railways all his life. With so many hopeful entrants, judging was done along the route and prizes awarded afterwards on the sports field. (*Charles Ashton*)

Illawalla, the luxury bungalow owned by Sir Walter de Frece, in the early 1900s. Famous stars like Ellaline Terry, Vesta Tilley (who became Lady de Frece) and Clara Butt stayed here while appearing at Blackpool's Winter Gardens, Opera House or Grand Theatre. At Christmas time it was sumptuously decorated and the 'waits', or carol singers, from local churches were generously rewarded when they sang for Illawalla guests. The next owner of Illawalla, the grounds of which stretched down to the River Wyre in Little Thornton, was Mr Broadbent, known locally as the 'Banana King'. Every day his liveried chauffeur, Hispano Suiza, standing smartly alongside his limousine, collected Mr Broadbent from the famous Club train which stopped at Poulton-le-Fylde station. The Club trains acquired this name because many businessmen travelled on them and enjoyed playing cards during the journey and so the carriages resembled clubs. The station catered for the dozens of excursion trains bringing visitors to Blackpool, especially during Wakes Weeks. The other well-known Club train, which went to Southport, was known as 'The Palestine Express' because many Jewish people travelled on it.

Opposite, below: Baines Endowed School sports day, 1965. The headmaster, Mr Jackson, is seated beside Mrs Hopkinson who has presented the prizes and has herself been given a bunch of flowers. Some of the lucky winners proudly display their books. Under James Baines's will, provision was made for the governors of the endowed school to partake of a good dinner every 2 February at the Bay Horse Inn, Thornton. Over a hundred years after the will was drawn up, a level crossing for the Preston & Wyre Railway was placed next door to the Bay Horse Inn, where Isaac Taylor was licensee. (*Sheila Isherwood*)

A noble Shire horse, decorated with rosettes, swags and horse brasses, a sturdy farm cart and a group of pretty girls participate in Thornton Gala, 1910. Everybody helped and looked forward to the great event year by year. The farmers lent fields, the grounds of The Towers (the local big house, now demolished) were available for children's sports and farm carts, handling manure one day, were scrubbed down and lavishly decorated the next. On the back of this photograph someone has written, 'Norah, front, second from horse'. (*Sheila Isherwood*)

Above: A postcard advertising the film *Esmeralda*, which was featured at cinemas along the Fylde coast in 1924. It starred Mary Pickford – she is the girl cowering at the piano. These early silent films were similar in theme and style to music-hall performances, and also played on the Victorian love of melodrama.
Right: The actress Livinia Boughey portrayed 'Mrs Dudgeon' at the Blackpool Grand Theatre in the early years of the twentieth century.

The promenade at Thornton-Cleveleys, 1937. This year Lord Stanley opened the Jubilee Gardens, which featured a paddling pool, tennis courts, pitch and putt and bowling green (Lord Stanley bowled the first wood). In the arena by the clock tower concert parties were held throughout the season, with performances by the likes of Charlie and the Follies and the Jolly Tars.

Besses o' th' Barn Band, 1906. They were regularly invited to Thornton and Fleetwood on important occasions and, for example, were present at the opening of the Whitworth Institute as town library. They were a particularly successful brass band and had begun playing in 1818 as Clegg's Red Band. In 1821 and on 21 June 1837, the day of Queen Victoria's coronation, they were judged the best band in a local competition. William Jones joined in 1830 at the age of twelve and died in 1891 having served for forty years as bandmaster.

Young Tomlinson and Shepherd wearing traditional Lancashire clogs, *c.* 1900. Photographs of classes of schoolchildren show that clogs and boots were general footwear from the 1870s onwards. At Marsh Mill Craft Village, Thornton-Cleveleys, there are regular demonstrations of the art of clog-making. Until machines took over, the clogs were made by hand, every process selected and worked by the clogger. Slater's Directory for Lancashire in 1882 lists ten boot and shoe manufacturers and three clog- and patten-makers for this part of the Fylde coast. In 1850 the most complete boot and shoe manufactory in the North of England was John Gorrill's, which produced a thousand pairs of boots every week. 'Brown seaside boots' of every variety cost *2s 6d* a pair! The nearest branch to Thornton was in Preston. Of the clog-makers in the Fylde the Clegg family had shops in Poulton, Kirkham, Fleetwood and elsewhere. Jonathan Clegg was the clog- and patten-maker for Bispham in 1880. (*Wyre Borough Council*)

Morris dancers and maypole dancers holding their ribbons attached to the maypole at Thornton Gala, 1910. In the foreground some elegant Edwardian costumes can be seen and an expensive-looking motor car, perhaps a Lagonda? At the 1927 Thornton Gala a great historical pageant was staged at 2 p.m., detailing the history of England in twenty tableaux. Marquees and swingboats were erected in Councillor R. Jenkinson's enclosure opposite the council offices, and there was dancing, a greasy pole and of course the crowning of the rose queen, with over 1,500 children taking part in the various activities. (*Charles Ashton*)

Cleveleys Hydro, 1912. Advertised nationwide as 'The Hydro of the summer and winter resort', it comprised a fully licensed hotel with an eighteen-hole golf course. At the time it was considered to be truly up to date with grass and shale tennis courts, all types of bath, including Turkish, foam and sunray, central heating, garage space for eighty motor cars and a resident orchestra. Cricket matches were held in the spacious grounds as well as tea dances and garden parties, which were very popular.

Bathers enjoying themselves on the sands with Cleveleys Hydro in the background, 1913. The latest fashions in bathing costumes and hats can be seen here. Pulled down in the late 1950s, the Hydro has been replaced with houses and bungalows. The flatness of the Fylde area has attracted people to retire here.

Dick Shepherd (1886–1923) stands outside his saddler's shop, 1912. These premises had also offered smithy and wheelwright's services in the nineteenth century. Elastic knee caps for horses, hunting, plain and ladies riding saddles, horse collars, harnesses, cart gears, whips, leathers, brushes and carpet bags were all obtainable from the saddler.

Opposite, above: A crowded street in Blackpool, 1912. When staying at Thornton it was usual to catch the tram down the coast to Blackpool. For the ladies Gouldens Limited, costumiers and furriers, was the shop to visit 'for London and Manchester fashions fresh from Paris!'. The number of people gathered outside the establishment may suggest that a celebrity is due to arrive at the Grand Theatre.

Opposite, below: The Sea Wall Swifts football team, 1950. David Cookson kneels in the centre with the football; Tom Ball and Eric Cranston are also in this group. The team played fixtures in Thornton and their home matches were played at the speedway ground. In 1887 the Fleetwood Rangers team started and during a London tour they beat Arsenal, Millwall and Chatham. Their centre forward was Sam Colley who declined an offer to sign for Blackpool, preferring to play part-time football and continue smack fishing.

Victoria Road East, Thornton, 1915. Many of these houses became shops. Thornton was originally a large township which extended for half a mile outside Poulton-le-Fylde to the port of Fleetwood. It contained 6,387 acres of the manorial lands belonging to Peter Hesketh, but by the 1880s the Fleetwood Estate Company was the chief landowner in the area.

Thornton for Cleveleys station, 1915. The Preston & Wyre Railway opened this line in 1840 with its terminus in Fleetwood. These platforms and the approaching steam train are long gone, and Ramper, as it was then called, closed down in 1843. By 1865, on the same site and in busier times, another station, Cleveleys, had been built. On 1 April 1905 the station was renamed Thornton for Cleveleys. During holiday seasons, crowds five deep lined the length of this platform and it was also regularly used by Rossall schoolboys.

Mary Nelson of Thornton on her wedding day, January 1926. Her wedding dress was grey-blue crêpe de Chine at a time when there was a wonderful choice of materials. The tiered dress (or 'frilled') was fashionable for ladies and little girls. Short skirts were all the rage as long, trailing gowns had disappeared ten years earlier with the emancipation of women during the First World War years. Mary was a trendsetter, and while she and a friend were on holiday in the Lake District seized the opportunity to have their hair 'bobbed'. Returning home, rather fearfully, to Thornton, they soon discovered they had set a fashion. Some of the girls sold their long tresses when they had their hair bobbed or had an 'Eton crop'. Others, like my mother, wrapped the long, glossy hair in silk and kept it for years. Mary was married at 8.30 a.m. at Christ Church, her father being a shy man who disliked any fuss. (*Sheila Isherwood*)

Thornton Tennis Club members, 1921. Of the three standing at the back, the third from left is John Jagger, headmaster of Beach Road Junior School. The six ladies are clad in fully fashioned silk stockings, cloche hats, one-bar leather shoes and pine-marten fur necklets and typify the style of the late 1920s and 1930s. (*Sheila Isherwood*)

Lord Street, Fleetwood, cluttered with logs from Alex Keay's sawmills following floods, October 1927. The flooding of the Fylde coast in the autumn of 1927 was the most devastating in living memory and it was the town of Fleetwood that suffered most. A Sea Wall Act had been passed by Parliament in the previous June but the wall had not yet been built when the seas roared in. Bispham escaped but lower-lying Thornton-Cleveleys was flooded up to the tram track, which at that time turned inland, and the whole coastline suffered storm damage.

Phyllis Edge, a Thornton girl who married a wealthy man and lived in a large house (now demolished) on School Road, 1919. They held tennis parties there in the glorious summers of the 1920s. Phyllis's husband owned the firm that made 'Dolly Blue' washing powder at the village of Backbarrow, now in Cumbria as a result of boundary changes. 'Out of the blue, comes the whitest wash' was their advertisement in the days before automatic washing machines. Housewives had 'coppers' to heat vats of water, 'possers' to plunge, which released dirt, and Sunlight soap and 'Dolly Blue', the latter in a cotton package with a little wooden handle to dip up and down in the water while the sheets bubbled, eventually to emerge dazzling white. (*Sheila Isherwood*)

Hodgkinson's Mineral Water Wagon decked out for another procession, 1925. On the left is Mr Gleeson, manager, and Bert Hockinhull, the driver, in flat cap. Hodgkinson's delivered mineral waters, soda syphons and vinegar around the old Fylde but were based in Fleetwood. Behind the wagon is the Whitworth Institute, Welsby's tradesmen's store and in the other direction the old Decimus Burton property, built between 1830 and 1840 when the town of Fleetwood was rising.

A family picnic at Stanah on the banks of the River Wyre, 1911. Left to right: Sam Nelson with Winifred Mary in front, Norah, Annie Scholes holding Arthur and Zillah, Grandma Scholes with Hilda Moorcroft in front and Mary Elizabeth Nelson with Stuart William in front. (*Sheila Isherwood*)

The inauguration of Thornton's electricity supply with the Revd E.G. King in the centre and Councillor Betney on the extreme right, 1926. The council celebrated its golden jubilee year in 1950 and was granted a coat of arms *terra marique* – 'by land and sea'. Thornton-Cleveleys Council used to hold an annual tour of the district inspecting footpaths, roads, gas works, riversides, electricity sub-stations and the promenade. The first sewers to be installed were part of a joint scheme for Thornton, Bispham and Carleton. In 1923 an application was made to the Minister of Health for £19,200 for sewerage work. This was deemed essential as during the nineteenth century waste was collected in cesspools, which caused outbreaks of scarlet fever, while at Thornton Endowed School diphtheria had resulted in the deaths of children, a source of great sadness to the community.

The Promenade, 1930. People congregated at the bathing area, there were donkeys on the beach and a moveable water slide, usually crowded, in the midst of the waves. The new Promenade cost £30,000 and took ten years to build, work commencing in 1927.

Lord Stanley unveils the memorial tablet at the opening of Jubilee Gardens, 1937. Councillor Rowbotham is on the left, wearing the Homburg hat, and had laid the foundation stone on 17 September 1927 when he was chairman of the council.

On the same day in 1937 Lord Stanley cuts the tape to open the new Promenade. Thornton-Cleveleys Brass Band played and tea for elderly residents was served at the Regal Hotel. The children were issued with free vouchers for amusements and a grand procession arriving via Carr Gate featured lifeguards, lifeboatmen and Miss D. Horrabin dressed as Grace Darling in a rowing boat. Thornton had come a long way since 1901 when it borrowed £436 to purchase a streamroller.

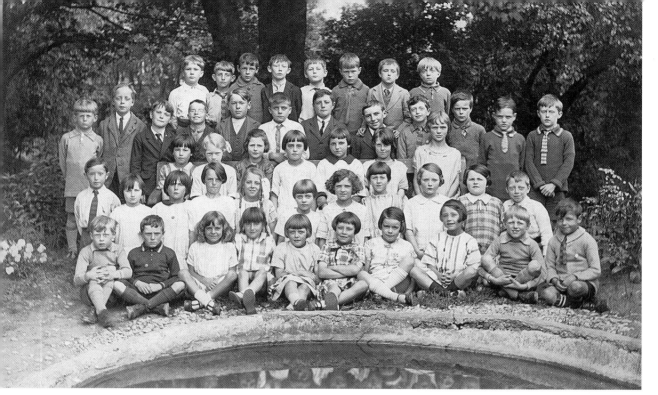

A class at Baines Endowed School, 1928. By this date the school leaving age had been raised to fourteen. Overcrowding, which had been severe for many years, was reduced, buildings were improved, discipline became less strict and self-expression was encouraged provided order was maintained. The new state grammar schools were built, which some of these pupils, via scholarships, managed to attend and to benefit from. On 31 August 1932 children over the age of eleven left to attend the new senior school built in Church Road. (*Joan Currie*)

White Hall on the banks of the River Wyre, upstream from Cartford Bridge, 1960. The Kirkby family, who by marriage gained the manor of Out Rawcliffe, set about building on the site in 1420, the last Kirkby selling his land to Thomas Westby of Mowbreck. The Kirkbys and Westbys were two important Fylde families and they in turn owned White Hall. It was George Westby who rebuilt White Hall as it is seen here. Many centuries ago a mill had stood here, but by 1860 the property had become a farm. In the 1950s, while farming, Mr Charnley discovered a tunnel leading from the house. He bricked it up, although there was a story connected with it that went back to the Civil War. It was said that after Cromwell routed the King's army at the Battle of Preston a member of the Westby family escaped on horseback and made for White Hall. There both horse and rider hid in the tunnel and evaded capture.

A Thornton Gala float, 1930. The local boys, including Douglas and Donald Currie, have donned false moustaches and Homburg hats. The cards they hold refer to local characters, including doctors and councillors. The job of the young man standing alongside the float was to lead the horse. (*Joan Currie*)

The District Nursing Association garden fête, 1946. This event was held annually to raise money for the association, members of which were all voluntary. Flower festivals were also run and the younger girls made buttonholes, posies in baskets and nosegays to swell funds. In the days before the NHS there were many money-raising efforts at Ashdell on Victoria Road, which was made available to the community for a variety of uses by the local council. The gardens were quite renowned. The association's committee is seen here, left to right: Mrs Downing (wife of the headmaster of Church Road Junior School), Dr Pennington (councillor), Mrs Keirby, -?-, Councillor Rowbotham, Mr W. Wright (clerk to the council) and Mrs W. Hopkinson (treasurer). (*Sheila Isherwood*)

Above: 2–6–0 Mogul Tank engine No. 90595 leaving Thornton station, 1960. *Below*: There were crowds of 'gricers' all the way when *Oliver Cromwell*, Britannia 4–6–2 Pacific engine No. 70013, thundered up at Thornton station, *c*. 1972.

The netball team at Palatine School, Blackpool, 1914/15. On the far right, kneeling, is Winnie Nelson. Fixtures were played against teams from Thornton. (*Sheila Isherwood*)

Thornton-Cleveleys beach at about the time of King George V's silver jubilee, 1935. Two heavy clinker-built boats took passengers on board via a moored wheeled trailer at certain times of the tide so that feet did not get wet. No lifejackets are apparent, but one wise girl has gone in her bathing costume.

Thornton Hall on Wyre Road, 1951. This fine house was owned by the Silcocks, a farming family, but was actually up for sale at this time, as was their famous herd of pedigree Dairy Shorthorn cattle. An earlier building, Brade's Thornton Hall, existed in the 1820s. The highway from Tarngate via Woodhouse Lane passed the gates and had to be kept in good repair by Thornton township. An arrangement to convey gravel by horse and cart was agreed with the surveyor who favoured local labour against that from further afield, which was more expensive.

Sundown on Morecambe Bay, 1937. Sunsets and sunrises seen from the coastal towns of Bispham, Thornton, Cleveleys and inland Poulton have long been famed. The bay, busy with shipping, had been surveyed by Staff Commander John Richards RN in 1871 (Chart 2010) and resounded in 1953, there having been a number of editions of the 1871 engraving. Lune Deeps, resounded by W.C. Jenks RN in 1937, carried a warning, 'Owing to the frequent changes in the Channels, Banks and Buoyage this chart must be used with caution . . . navigation in Morecambe Bay should not be attempted without a Pilot'.

The roots of the willow tree have undermined this old pebble wall at Rington Farm, 1962. Other structures in the Thornton area are crumbling but the bulldozing of pebble-built property is not an easy task.

A sixteenth-century Fylde cottage in Hawthorne Road. This one has had its thatch covered with corrugated iron, which happened all over Amounderness. As tiles and slates became common roofing materials it was less easy to find craftsmen qualified to thatch. Willow Cottage and Poolfoot Cottage, the latter on Crabtree Road, are the oldest remaining buildings in the area.

Below: Victoria Road West, Cleveleys, 1912. This street grew out of the old Ramper Road, the dyke designed to keep out the sea. Many of these properties were converted into shops and with the building of more houses and the increase in population a greater number of shops and tradesmen were required. Richard Gregson and Henry Jarvis were established grocers and Benjamin Warbreck dealt in sundries. William Stirzaker and Thomas Swarbrick still had plenty of business as blacksmiths. The number of boot- and shoe-makers had risen in Thornton with William Banks, Richard Butler, John Fenton and Robert Thomason all occupied in that trade. Everybody walked long distances and so footwear was of great importance.

Investigating the land at College Farm, 1980. This land was acquired by the firm Fairclough who proposed to build a housing estate there. This plan raised much opposition from nearby householders. There was much wrangling over many years but in spite of objections work began in 1995. The marshy nature of the land had from time immemorial attracted wildfowl, as many as 3,000 birds on occasion, among them pink-footed geese. Local residents and nature lovers protested that development would deprive the wild birds of their chosen habitat (particular sympathy was for a pair of swans who arrived every year in October). Before construction work commenced, a pylon had to be removed on account of the possible danger to health caused by its magnetic field. One thing the builders were not allowed to do was to scour the ditch bordering College Farm as this would have destroyed wildlife and plants. That was one battle the residents won. (*Robert Gibson*)

Opposite above: A scene from *Here We Come Gathering* staged at the parish hall, Thornton, by the Windmill Players, 14–17 October, 1954. The players are, left to right: Eric Gannon, Irene Chadburn, Wilf Roach, Audrey Stephenson, Ilfra Freebairn, William Croker, Dick Darlington, Robert Wylie, Pat Johnston. The Windmill Players were established in 1945 and have since produced about 160 plays, their forte being comedy and farce. Performances have been at the Thornton parish hall but more recently, because the hall is to be sold, the venue has switched to the lecture hall next door to the Lancashire Library. It is hoped that this building, dating from the mid-twentieth century, will be refurbished and extended, with extra accommodation to be built on the car park at the rear. Among the plays staged by the group are *A Man for All Seasons*, *Dry Rot*, *Blithe Spirit* and *Stepping Out*. The first production was *Ma's Bit o' Brass* and over the years the support of the late Bill Croker, Betty Horrocks, Wilf Roach and Pauline Elvidge has been invaluable in keeping a Thornton tradition alive. (*The Windmill Players*)

Opposite, below: The special party held in 1962 to celebrate the hundredth play presented by Thornton-Cleveleys Windmill Players since May 1945. Miss Violet Carson OBE (centre) attended to cut the cake (appropriately in the shape of a windmill) along with Mrs C. Bradshaw, widow of Jimmy Bradshaw, founder, and Bill Croker, chairman of the society. (*The Windmill Players*)

Brian Rawstrone's traction engine, 1965. Brian, from Thornton-Cleveleys and a descendant of Isaac Ball through the Cardwell family, restored this traditional traction engine from Ball's Yard at Wharles. He takes it for airings around the Fylde and delights children with its appearances at local events.

Adrian and James Strachan, at the front, enjoying a ride courtesy of the Fylde Society of Model Engineers, 1988. Originally called the Blackpool Society, it was formed in the early 1920s, the first track being built behind Marton Working Men's Club and Institute in Oxford Square in 1950. By 1972 planning was obtained to build a track behind the lecture hall in Thornton. When the ambitious Marsh Mill complex was begun by Wyre Borough Council in 1988, having been given notice to remove the track, the society was granted a site on the playing fields not far from Marsh Hill, as seen in this photograph.

3
Bispham & Norbreck

Jacob's ladder leading from the cliff to the shore at Bispham, 1927.

In this panel the initials are for Elizabeth and Edward Tinkler and their son Robert, and it was found at Ivy Cottage when the building was demolished in 1958. The cottage was a three-bay, cruck-style dwelling with buttery, parlour, soot-loft, fire-hood and clay and wattle walls. It had a wonderful open fireplace for peat or log burning and most impressively a massive thick wall, great at the base and tapering towards the roof space. The original building may have dated back to 1560 but in 1920 the owner, Mr W. Dawson of Bury Town Council, went further, claiming that Ivy Cottage was erected in the fourteenth century, which would make it over 600 years old. Mr Dawson ran a tea garden and café there, decorating the walls with spears, tribal carvings, knives and cutlasses from West Africa, brought home by his son. While they were refurbishing, the Dawsons discovered this panel, which measures 2 ft by 3 ft. They asked their next-door neighbour, 85-year-old Mrs Cookson, if she knew anything about it and she said, 'I remember my grandfather talking about the Tinklers when I was five but this family were not the first to live there'. The Bispham register of burials refers to a Tinkler in 1636, the grave being located in the churchyard of All Hallows.

This ancient cross in the churchyard of All Hallows, Bispham, could once have been a wayside or boundary cross. As was frequently the case, having been brought into the churchyard it was made into a sundial. The dial has long since gone, but on the stone shaft can be clearly seen the initials R.B., Robert Brodbelt, a seventeenth-century parish clerk who was reported to be something of a character and who supposedly cut his initials while resting on the steps. The lost dial, made by John Hebblethwaite, was dated 1704 with the motto 'Die dies truditor' ('Day treads on the heel of day') and the donor's initials I.H. (John Hull) deeply cut in Roman characters on the opposite side of the shaft. Record Office documents show Brodbelts to have owned land on the Banks of Bispham, including the windmill area, in the eighteenth century. Bispham windmill, no sign of which remains (nor does that of Rossall, which is recorded on old maps as being on the shore), must have had one of the best sites in the area, provided its sails could withstand the blasts of the Irish Sea and that the miller understood the art of controlling sails in contrary weather – perhaps this resulted in the windmill's demise.

The SS *Douglas*, viewed from Bispham cliffs, making her way to the Isle of Man, 1860. This early paddle steamer of the Isle of Man Steam Packet Company was built in 1858, although the firm had used a sloop of the same name under Captain Quayle in the 1830s. Trade had increased greatly and the company figurehead for SS *Tynwald* in 1845 was a triumphant full-length Manx Scandinavian king in armour.

Below: Edwin Waugh, who wrote a book about the Lake District and its borders in 1860. Staying at Norbreck, he devoted forty pages to the Fylde coast. Like Samuel Laycock, the Lancashire dialect poet and Waugh's great friend, he loved the area and wrote books and poems in the regional language. Waugh's description of 'Owd England' was 'sea-beaten patriarch, oldest inhabitant who went down to low water, shrimping daily', and of Norbreck he recalled 'grass-grown roads, pebble walls whitewashed and pretty gardens with cats lazily sunning themselves'. His book includes a fishing song written by William Garlick of Norbreck who was a weaver of the sail cloth known as 'Pow Davey'.

Above: In the company of 'Owd England', seen here, Waugh developed a liking for 'whilks' or sea-water snails. These thrived around Mussel Rock. At this time, tons of cockles were removed from cockle beds off Norbreck and Bispham. 'Owd England' was in reality Thomas Smith. To strike Old England was what farmers meant when they dug through sand and struck boulder clay.

The *Pearl*, which was wrecked at Norbreck on the night of 1 October 1895 in a north-west gale that destroyed numerous vessels along the coast. On the left of the photograph is thought to be 'the boathouse on the beach', which belonged to Norbreck Villa and was sold in 1897. This area has a history of disaster at sea. In October 1702 the *Employment* from Barbados, laden with sugar and cotton wool, 'suffered much hardship; with difficulty escaped and made for the Isle of Man but missing course, they ran under the red banks'. The ship was beaten to pieces by wind and waves 'but the cargo of sugar was saved, being put into Squire Fleetwood's barn and the cotton wool carted to Bispham Chapel' (these quotations are taken from the Revd W. Thornber's *History of Blackpool*). Afterwards it was sent to Manchester and sold for £200. In November 1844 a fishing smack, the *Jane and Lenny* from Port St Mary, was wrecked off Norbreck with the loss of four lives, the bodies being buried in Bispham church. 'How thankful I should be that the Banks at Rossall did not suffer', wrote the lord of the manor, Peter Hesketh, to Charles, his brother, after a particularly fierce storm on 15 January 1839. Mariners drowned at the foot of 'the Red Banks behind Rossall' were buried at Bispham church. As Sir Peter Hesketh-Fleetwood he spent so much money on town and railway building that he was forced to sell the contents of his home, Rossall Hall, and lease the building, which became a school for sons of gentlemen and the clergy, later known as Rossall School. Owning a third of the Fylde's coastline, he had proved to be a benevolent landlord, relinquishing the great tithes of wool and corn in the Thornton and Bispham areas for the benefit of his tenants. This took place at the time of the Commutation of Tithes when Schedules were drawn up, which gave details of the whole area.

Born on 30 April 1841, Mr R.S. Howarth, a master tailor from Manchester, always loved the sea. This photograph was taken at Yarmouth but when he was seventy-three he finally settled his family at St Anne's on the Fylde coast having returned year after year to Bispham, Cleveleys and Lytham St Anne's. *Below*: His daughters, Jessie, Ethel and Marjorie, are seated on a bench in the year of Mr Howarth's death, which occurred on 1 February 1928. (*Faith Bricher*)

Uncle Tom's Cabin, which was situated on the Norbreck Cliffs and was the earliest entertainment attraction of any size for visitors from Blackpool, 1892. In the late eighteenth century Margaret Parkinson of Bispham noticed how visitors enjoyed walking on the springy turf amid sea lavender, sea pinks, camomile and how they admired the sunsets and sea views. The air gave an edge to thirst and appetite so she set up a refreshment stall laden with ginger beer, nettle beer, ginger fairings, clap cakes and other sweetmeats. A wooden hut replaced the stall and the trip to 'Little London' became ever more popular. In later years, inspired by Harriet Beecher Stowe's book *Uncle Tom's Cabin*, the popularity of which had swept Britain, and by the addition of three figures reminiscent of the book, Margaret's enlarged premises took on the famous name of Uncle Tom's Cabin. The enterprise passed to Robert Taylor, a Blackpool lodging-house keeper, and went from strength to strength aided by the fact that the business had few competitors. A three-piece band was introduced so that dancing could take place. Parson Thornber mentions this – it was at such an event that he saw the beautiful girl Rose of Rossall. My grandfather became particularly interested in the site when a camera obscura was installed and my father, who became a professional photographer, was thrilled in the 1880s by James Wright's Photographic Studio, which was housed in a nearby building. A flight of steps down the cliff face led to a clean sandy beach, which was a great draw for families with numerous children. Alas, erosion by the sea literally resulted in 'Uncle Tom's' downfall.

Opposite, above: The figurehead of the barque *Abana*, which was washed ashore in 1894. 'In the early hours of 22 December 1894, in a great gale the 1,200 tons timber ship *Abana* foundered off the coast at Little Bispham and at ebb tide the ship's ribs are still to be seen in the sand. The alarm was raised by Robert Hindle of the Cleveleys Hotel. The 16 members of the crew who were all saved by the Blackpool Lifeboat presented him with the ship's bell. The *Abana* was built in New Brunswick, Canada, in 1874.' – this citation is engraved beneath the ship's bell, which today hangs in the north-west porch of the church that was built in 1916. It is rung at every service for the interment of ashes in the garden of remembrance. The captain of the *Abana*, Mr Danielson, also gave the ship's dog to the Hindles and the crew were taken to the Red Lion (known locally as the Red Cat) to be given refreshments and beds after their ordeal. The thrilling rescue by the lifeboatmen of the *Samuel Fletcher* is part of the folklore of this stormy region.

Opposite, below: Bispham smithy with the wheelwright's shop next door, 1886. Ploughshares and coulters were sharpened here and heavy carts mended. At the end of the nineteenth century Bispham was a small village of whitewashed cottages and farms mostly dating from the seventeenth century. The saddler's shop was the source of harness and tackle for the many horses. Along with the local store, which sold almost everything (Bispham's was well known for its treacle), and regular visits by the pedlar and travelling tailor in horse and trap, the village was self-supporting because the fields around grew corn and vegetables. The windmill was situated at Bank, a little further on than Red Bank. Records show that Bank was once known as the Cliffs of Egberg. Between the parish church and village centre was the bow-windowed Red Lion Inn, where the shipwrecked crew of the *Abana* thankfully recovered. Frederick Fitzroy Thompson was landlord – his son later on took over the Castle Gardens Inn at Carleton. Inland was Beryl Hill and Knowle Farm covering 200 acres from Bispham Road to the coast. The road from Warbreck village led to Knowle Farm where the Fielding family worked the land.

Ivy Cottage Tea Gardens, Bispham, early 1900s. From the late nineteenth century onwards thousands of people who stayed in Blackpool came in wagonettes or on foot to the tea rooms at Ivy Cottage, for Bispham was a favourite day trip destination, the village still being rural and a great contrast to noisy Blackpool. In 1871 the population of Bispham was only 536, by which time a temperance hall had been erected by subscription. The teetotallers favoured tea rooms and gardens, railing against the taverns and inns that supplied intoxicating liquors, so this may have contributed to the success of Ivy Cottage. Names associated with Ivy Cottage are Mr Nimrod Pilling and Mrs Harriet Campbell. Kate Greenhalgh is reported as being at Ivy Cottage, Norbreck, ten years earlier when Bispham was a township with Norbreck in the county council division of Fleetwood and Fylde Union – the area was then known as Bispham-with-Norbreck.

Bethel Chapel, 1880. The chapel was built in 1834 and before that meetings were held in a cottage where preacher Thomas Cooper was known to have held forth from about 1730 onwards. What Thomas Hardy might have called 'a group of noble dames' was known at one time in Bispham as the 'sod cutters' – armed with heavy farm spades they cut out an area intended possibly for Bethel Chapel. It was certainly for a place of worship.

All Hallows Church, Bispham, *c.* 1920. This was the mother church of Blackpool where all Christian weddings, baptisms and burials were held until Blackpool built St John's in 1821. The present All Hallows is the fourth church on the site and retains the red sandstone south doorway of the second church, which was built in Norman days. The penance stool and the old stocks were kept in the belfry. 'Fallen women' were called to sit on the penance stool in the body of the church to be rated by the preacher in front of the congregation. Rebuilt in 1881, the fourth All Hallows was designed to accommodate 300 people. The church in existence in 1296 was dedicated to All Saints. Richard Higginson gave money for rebuilding, providing a Free School and £40 a year towards the maintenance of a preacher.

An artist's impression of old Bispham village in the nineteenth century. Nowadays, apart from a tiny newsagent's shop, not one old building is to be found. One was preserved for some time following the 1937 road-widening scheme – Jimmy and Nibby Hornby's Tuck Shop where the lads of the village drank Vimto (hot in winter) and played cards. One shop originally had a communal oven where all the villagers had their bread baked on a certain day of the week.

One Ash Cottage, 1915. Like Rustic Cottage and Ivy Cottage, One Ash was a well-known 300-year-old dwelling, heavily topped with thatch and surrounded by shrubs and trees, its ash tree, like the one in Carleton village, being a landmark. At about this time, the wooden steps, Jacob's ladder, leading from the high cliffs to the shore, began to disintegrate.

Taken in about 1890, this photograph is a mystery but undoubtedly relates to Norbreck and Bispham. The oldest building on the boundary between the two areas was Cliff Cottage, which had a weaving shed attached. Cottages in Norbreck and Bispham had areas for the hand-loom weaving of a sail cloth known as 'Pow Davey'. Could this be the workshop built at Bispham for weaving linsey-woolsey, a material popular in the Fylde for women's clothing? John Duxbury and Thomas Lewtas had built such a factory. It is on record, but the partners went bankrupt. Hand-weaving in the cottages persisted and was referred to by Edwin Waugh in his journeys round Lancashire as he recorded dialects. He was impressed by the hard-working villagers: 'When Lizzy was churning in the dairy, granny was baking and Little Tom, the cow lad, had started early with a cart of coals for Poulton.'

Norbreck sands where some ambitious sand-castle building has been finalised and a well-wrapped-up toddler has probably tumbled over in the effort of paddling, 1906. This happy family group are wearing the fashions of a century ago. Is 'the fool on the hill' about to roll a boulder down on to the beach?

The postcard states that this is the cliffs at Blackpool, photographed in about 1914. On the reverse an advertisement urges people to 'Invest in Government Securities'. However, the area seen here was once part of Bispham. The 960 acres of ancient Biscopham extended to the pool, a peaty brown sluice that emptied into the sea from Marton Mere. This dark-coloured pool eventually became Blackpool, the confines of which spread as the resort became one of the most popular in Britain.

Another view of One Ash Cottage, which was issued as a postcard in the late 1920s. The next building on the right was the Manchester Bank, a private house. Nearby the old Bispham Endowed School was in the charge of John Danson and Gladys Coates, the Albion Inn changed its name to the Old England and the Red Lion Inn on All Hallows Road had thick bottle-glass bow windows. The latter was demolished in 1938.

The church and Church Cottages at Bispham, early 1900s. Church registers record people with names such as Cowban and Bamber, who resided at the Poole, or Le Pull, but were buried at Bispham. In 1549 there was a dispute over places in Bispham that included the Poole, but it was not until 1751 that the name Blackpool appeared on a map.

A lovely old postcard of the tramway station at Bispham, with one tram advertising 'Brilliant Illuminations', *c.* 1920. Even earlier the Blackpool Tramroad Company offered 'the cheapest and most exhilarating outing that can be obtained'. Cars left every quarter of an hour. John Cameron, secretary and general manager, came from the Isle of Man with a team of Manx men to work on the original construction and frequently walked the whole route to see that all was in order. The Camerons, who lived in Red Bank Road, attended regular Sunday worship with their large, well-dressed, well-behaved family who together filled two pews and made an impressive group.

An illuminated tram that passed along the coast from Starr Gate, South Shore, Blackpool, to Fleetwood, *c.* 1930.

Frederick Kemp, one of the original directors of the Fylde Waterworks, who lived at Bispham Lodge and is seen here in about 1860. In the early 1840s Kemp was also agent for Peter Hesketh, lord of the manor, and was heavily involved in the commerce of the district, including the North Lancashire Steam Navigation Company which in 1851 took delivery of 'a pair of Kemp's Marine boilers for the steamer Fenella'. The jubilee of the Fylde Waterworks took place on 22 July 1911, royal assent having been given to the necessary Bill in July 1861. Engineer Edward Garlick reported in October 1895, 'A new trunk main must be laid before long notwithstanding the proposed new service reservoir at the Knowle'. A 6-in main to Warbreck Hill had to be constructed 'to meet the growing demands of Bispham' from the 24-in main there, 'along the proposed Warbreck Drive, terminating near the Generating Station of the Blackpool and Fleetwood Tramroad Company'. By the 1930s the remarkable growth in the district resulted in the building of the water tower at Warbreck, which is now a notable landmark.

The Bungalow, Norbreck, where the Barlow family lived in the 1920s. This line of old thatched cottages underwent some changes over the years, for example, tall chimney stacks were added, dormer windows were installed and a more up-to-date porch was built, but they are still recognisable as typical old Fylde homesteads. When he stayed there in 1860, Edwin Waugh described Norbreck as 'a quiet little hamlet overlooking the sea, smelling of roses and cribs where oxen lie'.

The corner shop in Bispham village advertising Fry's pure cocoa and Spratt's patent dog biscuits, 1900. Almost every other commodity from oatmeal and treacle to fire lighters and paraffin could be obtained here. The decorative finger post on the far right directs people to the seashore and tram station.

This Fylde cottage was pointed out to visitors as being typical of its kind. John Bright, politician, may have spent time here besides staying at Woodbine Cottage, upon whose site a garage was built, one of the first on Victoria Road. Another famed Fylde cottage was known as Rustic Cottage. In 1921 Captain Preston bought it but it was knocked down in 1924, still with its thatched roof and ornamental arch of driftwood around the garden gate. The cottage adjoined Norbreck House, which was linked with stories of smuggling and was eventually demolished in 1932.

The porch of Norbreck Villa. This building, constructed in the mid-nineteenth century, remains and is located opposite the Victoria Hotel, which is now called the Mariners' Hotel. The Norbreck Hydro grew out of Hardman's Norbreck Villa. James H. Shorrocks, to whom the villa was leased, felt that there was potential in enlarging it and creating a huge hotel with castellated features, still visible today and possibly inspired by the gazebo at nearby Rossall Hall. Built at about the same time as Anchorsholme Hall, Eryngo Lodge, once a private dwelling, was licensed under Benjamin Corless Sykes to become Cleveleys Hydro. With its sea-water baths, golf course, music room, ballroom, lift and stage it was the height of luxury, yet could be enjoyed for just 7s 6d a day. Anchorsholme Hall eventually became a private hotel and flourished until 1948, but by 1967 it had been demolished.

Ivy Cottage, 1904. By this time its fame as a cosy café was spreading. On the back of this postcard Bessie writes: 'Had tea here yesterday.' On the far right is a poster encouraging visitors to visit the Furness district by sailing up the coast from Fleetwood. Furness Abbey was one of the local historic beauty spots and had been so since the 1830s, but it could be a choppy sail there.

King's Drive, Bispham, c. 1925. Set high up on the cliffs at Bispham and close to the trams, this area became as popular as Queens Drive, both having the great advantage of no risk of flooding but glorious sea views. The top of Red Bank Road by the tram station is the highest point along this stretch of coast. One jolly doctor advised influenza sufferers to 'go blow your brains out on the cliffs'. Wonderful sea air was thought to aid recovery after illness.

Norbreck looking south, 1960s. This view is much the same today, although back then one of the attractions on the breezy cliffs was crazy golf costing 6d a round. The ornamental shelters, these days somewhat dilapidated, were havens from the wind and rain. Norbreck also had its well-signed tram station on the successful tramroad that was completed on 19 May 1897.

Santos Dumont.

A postcard recording the first aviation meeting in England, held at Blackpool in 1909. The inset shows Monsieur Santos Dumont. From Bispham, Thornton-Cleveleys and Norbreck it was possible to gain glimpses of this event. It was in actual fact the second meeting as Doncaster had staged one three days before, but Blackpool, rarely beaten at the post, was the first to organise insurance and to be sponsored by the Aero Club. Blackpool's event was more spectacular but the weather was appalling. Wind and rain put both pilots and machines to the test. On the first day there were 120,000 spectators. The five British aviators were Roe, Singer, Charter, Mortimer and Neale, but the French team scooped the prizes. Henry Farman, an Englishman brought up in France, lost his machine in transit from Berlin. However, as world distance champion he was able to borrow M. Paulhan's Voisin biplane and, first in the air, he rose to 50 ft. Turning towards St Anne's, he was forced to alight 'owing to some slight defect'. Tools were brought and to the amazement of the crowd in trying again he completed the full circuit. Lancashire man, A.V. Roe, made a brave attempt and although travelling 300 ft, failed to take off. Another Englishman, referred to as 'the dark horse', fell into the sea at St Anne's! The show ended on 23 October in weather so atrocious that the organisers had to fly flags from Blackpool Tower indicating whether or not flying was in progress. Dumont's plane, seen to the left of his portrait, looks rather unsafe. (*Ron and Barbara Strachan*)

Palm Court, Bispham, dates from the 1920s when more ambitious hotels were rising to meet demand from holiday-makers. The enlargement of Norbreck Hall Hydro and Cleveleys Hydro bear witness to this. In 1910 at nearby Carleton Mrs Townsend advertised accommodation at Allendale, Bispham Road, but most visitors wanted to stay on the cliffs close to the sea.

The Vicarage, Bispham, 1910. This rambling Virginia creeper-covered building was home to the incumbents of All Hallows Church, Bispham, which at the time of this photograph was Canon Leighton. Canon Ward and Mrs Ward lived here in 1940 when a great snowstorm covered the country and the road to All Hallows had to be dug out by American soldiers. Snow reached towards the roof tops and blanketed the hedges.

The Gynn Inn, 1906. The Blackpool & Fleetwood Tramroad Company Ltd worked with the Gynn Estate Company Ltd, formed on 19 May 1897 by local businessmen, to improve the Fylde coastal area. The old inn was a favourite meeting place. During the eighteenth century on a particularly wild night a ship was saved by the innkeeper's daughter placing a lantern in a window. The cellars of the Gynn, however, were flooded with sea water on that night.

The cliffs at Bispham, 1913. At this time the area had a wilder, more natural look but erosion was considerable. Photographer Mr Lord of Poulton took this view of the crowded cliffs along with a series of others, all of which were on sale to visitors. As they came from smoky towns like Manchester and Bolton one can understand reactions such as 'This is a beautiful place, enjoying the sea air. Lots of wind!'

The village of Bispham viewed from Cliff Terrace, which was close to Red Bank Road, with the Manchester Bank and a knot of village children gathered, all eager to be in the photograph, 1928. It was probably winter or early spring as the trees are reasonably bare. In the summer roses and hollyhocks would have flowered in the tiny gardens bordering the cottages.

Old cottages in Bispham, c. 1900. Garden walls were made from cobbles taken from the seashore and they can still be seen here below the railings. Extra coats of whitewash were applied to garden and cottage walls annually, thatch was repaired and post arrived, via Poulton-le-Fylde, at 7.10 a.m. daily. Richard Cookson had run the post and money order office since 1892 and the Albion Hotel served as the posting house.

Cliff Place, Bispham, 1922. This development was the product of early building speculation and attracted retired people and families to seaside homes. One such was Miss Kay who lived at The Nook, Cliff Place. Thornton Urban District Council commissioned Maurice Fitzgerald to photograph the unmade state of roads as demand for houses could not keep pace with road surfacing.

Queens Drive, Bispham, 1954. This photograph reveals the growing popularity of the Fylde coast at this time and the many ambitious building plans being implemented to open up the area, as well as the improvements to the tram track connecting the town quickly and efficiently with Blackpool and Fleetwood.

The Lucas Holiday Camp at Norbreck was one of the earliest on the Fylde coast and is seen here in the 1920s. Run by its teetotal owners for young men, it was very popular and afforded workers a healthy holiday at very reasonable rates. Most visitors slept under canvas and there are postcards from the 1920s and 1930s showing orderly rows of tents, pitched close to the seashore where the Promenade was later built.

Opposite, above: The beach, Norbreck, 1906. Dunes, sea holly, sea pinks and marram grass controlled the blowing sands to some extent, but crumbling pebble walls eroded further as the sea advanced and the few unpaved tracks leading to the shore contributed to the coast's wild appearance. Nature in the raw appealed to those people wishing 'to get away from it all'.

Opposite, below: Alexandra Road, 1922. Mrs Dyson lived at no. 3 and took in visitors. Henry Thistleton, born in 1850 and at the time this photograph was taken one of Bispham's oldest inhabitants, lived at no. 12. Henry, who died in 1936, could recall the early days of village life. Abraham Barlow, coal merchant, another lifelong resident of the area, gave £1,000 to found the Abraham Barlow Trust. Poet Vernon Scannel and oboist Evelyn Rothwell, wife of Sir John Barbirolli, visited Bispham in the 1970s by arrangement of the trust.

The swimming baths at Norbreck Hydro, 1950. These were opened in the winter of 1931 by Councillor G.N. Hardcastle when T.H. Shorrocks was manager of the establishment. The pool, measuring 60 ft × 27 ft, had a mosaic floor made up of turquoise and amethyst tiles. The walls were pink-cream tinted. All materials used were state of the art and this attracted visitors from inland.

A whetstone for sharpening knives, spades and plough coulters that was thought to have been used at Knowle Farm, 1957. In 1898 T.W. Fielding was farming there. Knowle House was the home of Sir Wilfred Ashley, whose beautiful daughter Edwina became Lady Mountbatten. The Knowle estate extended to the cliffs and there were plans to build villas on part of the estate but these did not materialise.

This 1959 photograph reveals that Ribble bus services had arrived, roads had improved and many of the old cottages remained. Thatch had been replaced with tiles and the oldest cottages, including the smithy, were marked down for demolition. In February 1937 a couple of 300-year-old cobble-stoned cottages and a shop at the junction of Red Bank Road and All Hallows Road had to be knocked down as part of a road-widening scheme. Mr J. Parkinson, for many years an inhabitant of the village, sadly recalled a cottage seventy years before when 'the cottager kept his own cow and shippon'. Red Bank Road was so named because of its proximity to the 'red cliffs' formed by a type of marl or clay the colour of which washed into the sea with each tide. For more than a hundred years Bispham had only one road through it from Hoo Hill to Cleveleys, as long before this the sea road from Norbreck had been swept away.

The Lower Walk, Promenade, Bispham, 1952. Much work had taken place here to retain the cliffs and make walkways down to the sea. The local girls used to call this 'the monkey walk' – possibly because it resembled the monkey house at the zoo!

BY TENDER,

OR A TERM OF YEARS,

FROM CANDLEMAS NEXT,

FOLLOWING CLOSES OF

ABLE, MEADOW, AND PASTURE

AND,

SITUATE IN THE TOWNSHIPS OF

TON AND BISPHAM-WITH-NORBRECK,

in the occupation of MR. JOHN SHAW.

				Quantities in Statute Measure.		
	IN CARLETON		A.	R.	P.	
	LOT 1.		A.	R.	P.	
Field			10	1	11	
	LOT 2.					
Field			9	2	11	
	LOT 3.	A.	R.	P.		
Marled Field		10	0	29		
		1	0	9		
		5	3	0		
					16	3	38
	LOT 4.					
		4	1	23		
		6	1	22		
					10	3	5
	LOT 5.					
ecar Meadows			2	3	39	
	LOT 6.					
			3	3	39	
	LOT 7.					
		3	3	12		
		4	2	11		
					8	1	23
	LOT 8.					
			1	2	38	
	IN BISPHAM-WITH-NORBRECK					
	LOT 9.					
pham Meadow			5	2	9	
	LOT 10.					
otment			9	0	20	
	LOT 11.					
otment			4	0	32	
	LOT 12.					
o arts, and Waste			6	0	0	

A poster from the late nineteenth century showing closes of arable land in Carleton and Bispham-with-Norbreck. Lot 5, Risecar Meadows, refers to 2 acres, 3 rods and 39 poles, which were nineteenth-century archaic land measurements. Mr John Shaw lived at Bridge Farm in Great Carleton at this time.

Ryescar Farm on Bispham Road, 1973. There had been a farm on this site for centuries and it is recorded with a variety of spellings – Ryescarre, Riscow, Riseka. Biscopham and Norbrec are listed in the Domesday Book, 1086. Boundaries have changed with Layton, Warbreck, Anchorsholme and Blackpool once being part of Bispham. In 1883 the detached portion comprising Bispham Hawes was added to Layton. Great and Little Carleton were also involved in these alterations but in the 1970s local government reorganisation changed the situation again. Ryescar Farm is so old that it must have been affected by these movements of land.

This tram is Dreadnought 59, which took part in the twenty-tram grand centenary cavalcade on 29 September 1985. The strip of Fylde coast passing through Bispham and Norbreck from Blackpool to Fleetwood lay undeveloped until 1896 because the Lancashire & Yorkshire Railway Bill of 1864 was rejected and Fleetwood Tramroad Company under the 1896 Act was to construct a double-track electric tramroad from the Gynn to the North Euston. Eventually forty-one single-deck bogie electric tramcars were running, fifteen of which were enclosed saloons. The summer cars were open-sided, resembling those that operated on the Manx Electric Railway; small toast-rack trams did 'circulars'. In the 1920s minerals and goods were carried which necessitated a mineral sidings at Thornton Gate. In 1902–4, the heyday of the Dreadnoughts, John Cameron advertised the 'new coast tram road, for those in search of health-giving breezes free from dust and smoke. Fare sixpence'. The old company box cars had a large oil lamp mounted at the front and no metal guards, which in the early days led to accidents. When Blackpool's boundaries were extended the corporation took possession of the tramroad on 31 December 1919, and John Cameron received £10,000 in compensation.

The remains of the *Abana*, which was wrecked in 1894, stranded off Norbreck, its full length revealed from time to time by stormy seas, 1988. This photograph was taken after a storm when shifting sands revealed more than usual and showed what a large barque it was. On that night in 1894 the sands froze and there was snow on the shoreline. Also as a result of the 1988 storm the possible remnants of three fishing smacks, *Mayflower*, *Surprise* and *Petrel*, lost in the storm of 2 October 1895, came to light. However, remnants of masts and timbers were quickly lost again beneath shifting sands.

Norbreck Castle Hotel, 1978. This establishment grew out of Norbreck Hall Hydro. Mr T.G. Lumb, a businessman, determined to open up 'the wilds of Norbreck'. He also persuaded the famous architect E.L. Lutyens to design a 'cottage exhibition' in the area he hoped would become 'the city of the Fylde'.

Norbreck Hall Hydro with some early motor cars parked outside, 1920s.

Vintage Austin car YW 6916 en route to the veteran car rally at Norbreck Hydro, 1986. Peter is at the wheel with Alice beside him, both of whom were jazz enthusiasts and visited the coast for concerts.

A Fleetwood Motor Passenger Carrying Company Limited vehicle, early 1900s. Occasional trips were made to Bispham and Norbreck when visitors asked to see 'a real Fylde village'. In 1821 Bispham with Norbreck housed only 63 families comprising 323 persons, while Layton with Warbreck had 130 families. Of the total of 193 it was recorded that 177 of these were employed in agriculture or fishing.

4
Villages

A road-roller, works number 1352, belonging to Fleetwood Urban District Council and built by Thomas Green in 1888, seen here in 1899. The driver is J. Cardwell.

A seventeenth- or eighteenth-century oval stone engraved with an eye. Discovered in the rubble of a barn in Mill Lane, Hambleton village, this is almost certainly a hag stone. Country people placed these stones in their cottages, shippons and barns to ward off witches. Originally coloured with dyes made from mosses and lichens, traces of colour can still be identified on this hag stone.

Pye's eighteenth-century farm at Marshaw, 1906. Like Porter, Pye is a common name in the old Fylde. The Pye family, like the Winders, are numerous and representative of 'Old Wyresdale'. In 1863, at the age of fifteen, Catherine Winder worked a sampler, which is now kept at Woodlands where Catherine Tallentire, a descendant, lives. Many of the Wyresdale farms have carved, dated cupboards and Gornall's farm cupboard is dated 1678, which makes it older than the stone-built farm itself. The tree seen here is no longer standing and deep snowfalls like this one are no longer common.

The eighteenth-century dovecote in the grounds of Lytham Hall. The earliest pictorial reference to Lytham Hall was in 1600 when Sir Cuthbert Clifton was squire. Between 1757 and 1764 Thomas Clifton rebuilt the structure, employing the famous architect John Carr, of York. The dovecote, its brickwork in keeping with the hall, supplied fresh meat in winter, a time when most beef and lamb had to be slaughtered or salted down as winter feed was scarce. As can be seen, today the dovecote is in good condition, in contrast to the ruinous Shepherds Lodge in Big Wood. (*Ron Loomes*)

Robert Hesketh, aged four, outside Cardwell Farm, 1892. This photograph was taken by Mr W. Dandy. At a tender age country boys became accustomed to farm animals and the girls were trained in dairy management. Indeed these subjects, as well as gardening, were part of the school curriculum in a mainly rural area. Note the cobblestones in the yard and the horse fitted with 'blinkers' to shade its eyes. These were always used when visiting the windmills as the horses tended to shy at the moving sails, and in some cases horses had to be blindfolded. (*Robert Gibson*)

Isaac Ball, 1931. He was born in 1859 and lived to the age of eighty-four.

The Ball family, 1896. At the back is William, with Peter beside his father and Thomas sitting on the grass. Annie is the girl in the white dress beside her mother, Jenny, and the two older girls at the back are Betty and Nellie. In the early years of their marriage Jenny and Isaac walked from Banks, Southport, to Lytham, crossing the River Ribble on the ferry or by fording it. They set up a threshing and rolling business with Isaac's brother John at Wharles village. The whole enterprising family played an active part for there were eventually thirty-five traction engines and road-rollers working in the Fylde and up and down Lancashire. When William married he joined his Uncle John Ball at Forton, again helping with the threshing business, which he took over in 1924 as John had no children to inherit. When Isaac Ball died in 1943 it was his third son, Thomas, who managed the firm at Wharles. (*Robert Gibson*)

Doctor Hugh Court, family doctor, 1890. Although based at Kirkham, he travelled far into the Fylde visiting remote farms and homesteads. He and Mr I. Ball were the first two men in the Fylde area to acquire motor cars. Doctor Court's vehicle was a bull-nosed Morris. Much-loved and respected, he was always referred to by grateful 'Fyldeans' as 'a grand, old family doctor'.

A lady from Westby with her daughter complete with dolly, photographed in a fashionable St Anne's studio, 1903. The Grapes Inn, not far from their home, was in those days called Dumpling Inn because of an annual feast of stew and dumplings held there. A character called Little Tommy, the parish clerk of Wrea Green, walked this area wearing blue stockings and knee breeches. Even at the age of eighty he could still manage a walk of 20 miles. He was well known, possibly by this lady, in the days when 'everybody knew everybody else' in the villages.

Above, left: This unusual inn sign, weighing 300 cwt, which was from the Saracen's Head Inn at the Over-Wyre village of Preesall, is seen here in 1909. In the nineteenth century this heavy stone created a bulge in the wall above the inn door and had, for safety reasons, to be removed. The inn figures in the crime story *Death Drops the Pilot*, which was written early in the twentieth century. *Above, right*: Mrs Ann Smith and her dog Lassie, residents of Fernbreck Cottages, Preesall, with the inn sign, 1937. Ann, who worked at the inn as a girl, took pity on the carving that nobody wanted and had it placed in Jim Nicholson's garden at Fernbreck Cottages. 'Big Head' was what the country boys called it and leaning their bicycles against the head, they damaged its nose. Mrs Belle Nicholson came to the rescue with a 'nose job' but the day dawned when a subsequent brewery wanted the Saracen's Head back and it was returned to the inn yard in the 1970s.

Opposite, above: The Pack Horse Inn, Stalmine, 1872. Mr Isaac Crowe, landlord, and his second wife are standing by the entrance to the pub with Mrs Porter, of gypsy stock, and her rag cart (the names of the other lady and child are not known). In the course of its long history this inn lay empty for three years. There had been business for this establishment and the Seven Stars (so called because of the seven stars above the altar in the church next door), which also provided refreshment for wagonette parties and itinerant travellers. When there remained only trade for one, the brewers, Catterall and Swarbrick, took the Pack Horse's licence away. The last tenants were Mr and Mrs Crowe. In the busy days Mr Danson's smithy in their inn yard had been the meeting place for farmers to bring their mares for mating with stallions. For a hundred years the Porter family (this was a common name in the Fylde), of the Seven Stars, had run the post office for the village. After three years they decided to turn the Pack Horse into the post office. Wild life had moved into the ancient inn – a rabbit's nest was found in the rusty barred grate. However, a spick and span, if quaint, post office and village shop emerged and to this day the line of measures for gin, rum (and porter!) hang above the counter in descending order of size. The Mrs Porter of the crinoline skirts and rag cart had started out with a large basket in which her wares were carried. She walked miles, as far afield as Poulton and Blackpool, like Sabina Gallagher who sold watercress, 'brothers or sisters of the road', a hundred years ago and more.

Opposite, below: Garstang village, 1906. This is the top end of High Street outside Bartlett's Tea Shop and it is possibly a Thursday market day as there is a trestle table in the road with a mound of used clothing for sale. Harrison's saddler's shop is across the road, evidence that the horse was still indispensable. However, bicycles are obviously beginning to make an appearance.

The Fleece Inn at Dolphinholme, 1933. This ancient hostelry was a welcome stop in the days of the pack-horse trains, when hundreds of mules and donkeys carried great weights on their backs, supplies for the busy towns and for Dolphinholme mill. The outside flight of steps – the handrail has been added since – leading to the upper storey would have been used by the men in charge of the pack horses. This mode of transport from a century ago explains the number of inns in the area with the name Pack Horse.

Preesall village, 1907. The round building in the centre called Rose Cottage was built as a toll house. The Saracen's Head Inn was located nearby. In front of the inn a dancing bear used to perform as part of its tour around the Fylde villages. The bear and its keeper slept together in barns and stables on the route. A tightrope walker from Lancaster visited when Tosset's Feast (Tosset was the local name for Oswald, patron saint of the church, and tossets were sugary cakes) was held and he performed on a high wire stretched from the Saracen's Head to a building across the road (The Round House). The terrace of Fernbreck Cottages was built for the salt-mine workers from the Preesall pits, which, in later years, caused alarming subsidence. On 28 June 1933 the earth opened up to swallow half an orchard, farm buildings and paths and this was just the beginning. During the next three months intermittent subterranean rumblings and roarings persisted as the ever-hungry black hole grew. Naturally, the villagers were scared. Preesall village school, endowed by the Hesketh family, was built in 1695.

The Knott End & Garstang Railway dinner on 8 July 1927. In 1908 this country line issued an illustrated penny guide which ran to fifty-seven pages. This was a most enterprising gesture for the directors had had to put up with much ridicule as there were frequent delays and shortage of railway stock. The Revd Mr Bannister declared that it was called Knott End because it did not end. It just petered out in a muddy field and trains tottered along so slowly that passengers, said the clergyman, could get out and pick flowers on the way and be in no danger of missing their train stop. One over-worked engine, *Hebe*, was reclaimed as it had not been paid for but the directors went ahead with their celebratory dinner, full of plans for 'unique tours in the Fylde and Over-Wyre district'. Knott End's general store was at Highfield House, belonging to Mrs Taylor, and the village's main link with civilisation was the *Wyresdale* ferry boat across the river to Fleetwood.

American millionaire Mr Prescott Bigston changing horses at the Eagle and Child Inn, Garstang, during his tour of England, 28 June 1911. The craze had hit wealthy Americans not only to visit England but to tour in the romantic style of driving four in hand. To relive the old coaching days was an expensive indulgence with many horses involved and frequent stops at inns. The fabulously wealthy Alfred Vanderbilt loved horses and English coach roads. In 1907 he came with twenty-seven horses, his most famous team being (V for Vanderbilt) Viking, Venture, Vanity and Vogue. Mr Bigston came to Garstang in similar flamboyant style, creating headlines for the *Garstang Courier* and headaches for local suppliers. With nine companions, a coachman in 'Olde English' costume, frock coats, top hats, knee breeches, the ladies dressed for English weather in long ulsters and hats tied on with gauze, he had the 'works', including the long brass coach horn which heralded noisy arrivals and departures. However, his desire to buy the enormous set of antlers above Jem Stuart's Horns Inn at Garstang was not requited. They were not even for sale for 100 guineas!

The fireplace of the Waggon and Horses Inn, 1921. This range and the reference to 'the fire that never goes out' are typical of old Fylde, where it was considered unlucky to allow the fireplace to cool to grey ashes. The idea went back hundreds of years when the yule log was brought in to be kindled from the last of the burning faggots of the old year. When people moved from cottage or farm in Bleasdale and Wyresdale they took the burning embers in a metal bucket and used them as the beginnings of fire in their new home. So dependent on peat, wood or coal fires for heating, cooking and drying were these people that the symbolism of an unfailing source of warmth was not lost upon them. Note the primitive fire oven for bread or 'batch baking', the soot-black kettles and oil lamp.

Girls from the villages of Treales and Roseacre having just taken part in the Whitsuntide walk, 1900. They include, third from left at the back, Ethel Richardson, third from left middle row, Madge Davis and, sixth from the left, Jenny Hesketh. On the front row in the middle is Elizabeth Shorrocks and third from the right is Katie Massam. It was a tradition to have a new white dress, mob cap or hat and shoes for this event every year. (*Robert Gibson*)

Mr and Mrs Robert Gibson of Thornton-Cleveleys, *c.* 1930. The lady in this photograph contracted typhoid fever as a girl at Dingle Farm, Newton. She survived and lived until she was nearly a hundred but her hair turned snow white. Born Jennie Nellie Shorrocks, with her sister and brother they all lived at Blake Hall Farm, Goosnargh, where the children searched in vain for the priest hole reputed to be contained within the building and the underground passage leading to St Mary's Church. It is said that General Oliver Cromwell slept at Blake Hall before the Battle of Preston in 1648.

Betty, one of the four daughters of Jenny and Isaac Ball, 1900. She used this horse and trap to travel between farms and later became known as 'Grandma Shorrocks'. Isaac became such an important figure and such a character that he was universally known as 'Owd Isaac'. Betty delivered bailing wire and binder twine (the latter becoming colloquially known as 'Old Isaac'). And she collected the money, in gold sovereigns, in a leather Gladstone bag, which is still preserved today by Mr Robert Gibson, a descendant, in Thornton-Cleveleys. In 1904 there was a drama at Shorrocks Farm, where Grandma Shorrocks lived with her husband James. They were forced to move out when a younger brother claimed the tenancy of Shorrocks Farm upon the death of their mother on 1 January. The couple moved to Nook Cottage, Town End, Wharles. (*Robert Gibson*)

Tom Ball, Jack Rawstrone and Sammy Cardwell alongside the *Mauretania*, which belonged to Isaac Ball, 1901. At one time Isaac employed so many workmen they formed a football team! When not threshing corn, this traction engine could be converted for crushing stone and tar-spraying farm roads but by 1903 the first road-roller improved on this. As a result six more were ordered and put to work as far off as Barrow-in-Furness. Lancashire County Council gave the firm contract work. The line-up of engines in the yard at Wharles was impressive. In 1956 a disastrous fire caused great damage and Isaac was thought to have died of a broken heart. As the years went by the rusting remains were sad reminders of his glory days when thirty-five farmers needed him in Treales, Wharles and Roseacre alone. (*Robert Gibson*)

Another of the famous road-rollers, once so familiar in the Fylde, with Tom Ball at the wheel, 1916. Tom had an excellent training at Vulcan Motors, Crossens. Motor engineer and committed steam-engine man, he would not allow (as has happened at Forton) any steam traction engines to be broken up. It is thanks to Tom that so many engines have been preserved. (*Robert Gibson*)

Jessie Hall and her father Edwin with another form of transport in the Lytham area, 1908. The family lived at Crumpsall, Manchester, but settled happily in the Fylde. Clothes-conscious (witness Jessie's beautiful Edwardian hat and tailored suit) and food-conscious, they were vegetarians at a time when it was not generally popular. Indeed some adherents were labelled cranks but the Halls and Howarths lived to healthy old age on a meat-free diet. (*Faith Bricher*)

The Treales morris dancers with their schoolmaster, Mr Stephenson, 1900. The girls are all holding their morris sticks, which were very much part of the dance. Back row, left to right: first Alice Marquis, second Alice Hall, fifth Ethel Richardson; middle row: first Jenny 'John' Hesketh, second Jenny 'Dick' Hesketh; front row: second Nellie 'John' Hesketh. The middle names of the three girls are those of their fathers, given to them in order to distinguish them within large families, which were often related in farming communities.

Singleton Gala, 1935. This was a very special year as it was George V and Queen Mary's silver jubilee. The newly crowned queen and her retinue represent another Fylde tradition, the holding of annual galas, originally called Club Days.

Mrs Jenny Ball wearing a hand-crocheted silk top and favourite locket in the garden of Inverness House, Long Lane, 1925. The wife of Isaac Ball, she helped to build up the family business based in the village of Wharles. This bill from W.D. Dobson was for new furniture and included a sideboard made to Jenny's design, a handsome piece of furniture still in use today having been passed down to a grandson in Thornton-Cleveleys. It cost £20 and a piano stool was upholstered for 8s.
(*Robert Gibson*)

Residence: 26, BOW LANE.

JOINER AND CONTRACTOR.

❖

MAKER OF ALL KINDS OF FURNITURE.

EUSTON STREET,

Preston, *Aug 31* 192*5*

Mrs Ball

To **W. D. DOBSON, Dr.,**

CABINET MAKER AND UNDERTAKER, &c.

To Settee Upholstered in Tapestry	19	15	·
2 Divan Easy Chairs at £9-14-6 each	19	9	
2 small Mahogany Chairs	5	10	·
Re-upholstry Piano Stool		8	·
Axminster Carpet 4 yds × 3 yds	13	4	
Re-Polishing Piano	3	3	
Mahogany Sideboard	20		·
Oval Mirror & fittings	2	5	·
Mahogany Fire Screen		15	·
Mahogany Occasional Gate Legged Table	4	5	·
	88	**14**	**·**

Received with thanks
Sept 5
W D Dobson

The 'Sunbeams of Jesus' and the 'League of Nations' tableaux parade at Freckleton Gala, 1920. The revellers were unaware of the terrible tragedy that was to befall their community on 23 August 1944 when an American bomber crashed on the village school at Freckleton. Freckleton village is mentioned in the Domesday Book and the name has been spelled in a number of different ways over the years. (*Robert Gibson*)

Janey Halstead, one of the benevolent white witches of the Fylde, 1913. The belief in malevolent witches persisted for a long time. They were thought to turn milk sour and make horses go lame but white magic was curative and Janey was known for her power to get rid of warts. The magic involved a piece of notched firewood and through each notch was threaded a piece of cotton representing a wart. The wood was then hurled into a spot where it would never be disturbed and as the threads rotted away and disappeared so did the warts. From all accounts recalled by country folks, it worked! The homely remedies of white witches were appreciated especially if it meant there was no need to call the doctor. (*Robert Gibson*)

Annie Ball, who became Mrs Dick Hesketh of Skippool Farm, photographed in Douglas, Isle of Man, 1912. The Balls holidayed on the island, Grandpa Ball having a season ticket issued by the Isle of Man Steam Packet Company so that he could go many times during the good weather. The boats sailed from Fleetwood, which was handy for Fylde folk. (*Robert Gibson*)

George Coxhead stands in one of the fields at Shorrocks Farm with his pride and joy, two Shire horses, 1918. On the left is Boxer and on the right is Prince. Rossall, Garstang and Poulton-le-Fylde were, at one time, well known for good horseflesh and regular fairs for the sale of horses were held in Poulton Square and Garstang High Street.

At the door of this old thatched cottage is three-year-old Sara Hesketh, 1904. Some of the cottages in the area were built in the mid-seventeenth century. This one at Moorside, Treales, has had an extension built and a tiled roof added later, the roof of the original, main cottage, being of thatch.

Mrs Fisher and little Eileen Fisher of Treales Mill, 1930. Every little Fylde schoolboy and schoolgirl in the 1920s and 1930s would be sure to learn by heart Henry Wadsworth Longfellow's poem about the windmill, it being so apt for 'Windmill Land', as the Fylde was known. In its heyday forty windmills had their sails a'clacking so why not recite, with some fervour,

> Behold, a giant am I
> Aloft here in my tower,
> With my granite jaws I devour,
> The maize, the wheat and the rye
> And grind them into flour.

The tower mills of the Fylde were indeed giants. At the time of this photograph, from Warbreck Road, between Blackpool and Bispham, it was possible to see five windmills. (*Robert Gibson*)

Sisters Agnes and Constance Stirzaker with a friend from Skippool on holiday at Blackpool or Southport, early 1920s. FY1361, a mock-up of a bull-nosed Morris motor car, would seem to indicate the novelty and interest stirred at that time when few real examples were to be seen on the streets. (*Robert Gibson*)

Below: The bonnet of this empty charabanc displays the famous brass Leyland nameplate, 1931. Many such vehicles were acquired in the Fylde area to supersede the wagonettes, for it was good business to take visitors and holiday-makers into the country. Six banks of seats, each with space for four or five passengers, made for a jolly ride in the open air and, should it rain, a protective if cumbersome folding hood was erected. Fitted with running boards for easy access, TB 1022 on trip PTN 1470 is waiting for the passengers to return and the charabanc driver to finish his home-brewed beer. (*Robert Gibson*)

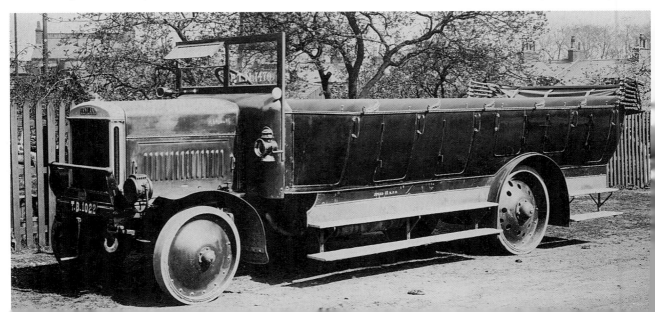

The Jolly Ollies, a group of young men from Bamber Bridge who enjoyed themselves giving concert parties in the Preston area, outside the entrance to Cuerden Park, 1908. They also went out to Garstang, a favourite time being Thursdays because that was when the market was held. Tom Broadley, Walter Billington, Bob Buck, Dick Yates, Sid Brown and Norman Hilton are among the group.

Miss Lawrenson's private school, Wesham near Kirkham, c. 1909. A number of so-called 'dame schools' proliferated to which the wealthier farmers sent their daughters as fee-paying pupils. In some cases boarding was offered. It is apparent from this photograph that part of Miss Lawrenson's timetable for scholars included housewifery. All the props of laundry work are on display except the bar soap. Note the two girls at the front in traditional Fylde sun-bonnets. (*Robert Gibson*)

Ladies at the Treales Women's Institute, displaying the many items of basketwork they have made for sale, *c.* 1920. The pieces include trays, waste-paper baskets, canework bowls and fire screens. In the early years of 'jam and Jerusalem' many homely skills were encouraged which proved invaluable during the two world wars and particularly in the raising of happy families. Included in the back row are Miss Jane Sanderson (second from left) and the Cowburn sisters (third and fourth from left). (*Robert Gibson*)

Nateby Agricultural Show, 1917. Mr T. Watson is holding the stick and his wife stands next to him with Mr and Mrs Shorrocks on the right, all of whom were interested in farming and the land. Mr Shorrocks managed farms in the Garstang area for Mr Watson. Dairywomen who, in proportion to the number of cows they had, made the greatest quantity of cheese annually could win £3 at the Nateby Agricultural Show. The latest farm machinery, such as Finlayson's Patent Harrow, was on display. At the Royal Lancashire Show in 1902 Isaac Ball had a large stand and showed off four Burrell traction engines – and he managed to sell two of the monsters.

Singleton village service station, *c.* 1918. The sign reads 'Agricultural engines. Shoeing & General Smiths'. The primitive petrol pump served the few motorists around at that time, but the main business was still for Billie Haslam and John Willie Jackson, blacksmiths. The building on the right is the smithy.

St Anne's Church, Singleton, 1909. The church was consecrated on 12 July 1860. The garden leading to the lych gate was well tended, its box hedges clipped and a herb garden maintained. Woodplumpton churchyard contains the eighteenth-century grave of a Fylde witch, Meg Shelton, feared in Singleton for so much malevolence that a huge boulder weighs down the grave to prevent her escaping. According to the Singleton miller and local farmers this is supposed to have happened three times.

Lytham Hall at Ballam, 1938. It was referred to as 'a sad house' in 1933 because it was shuttered and empty, but has come to life in recent years through the efforts of the Friends of Lytham Hall. The squire during the late nineteenth century was John Talbot Clifton, who spent much of his time in the distant lands of Africa and Peru. William Rufus having bestowed 10 carucates of Fylde land on a Clifton knight who had served him well, the family could trace an unbroken male line back to 1060, but few were 'stay-at-homes'. Supervising tenants and land did not appeal. After being given the freedom of Lytham St Anne's, Talbot bought Kirkham Castle on the Isle of Islay, to seek 'that peace which civilisation does not hold for me'. The hall, designed by the famous architect John Carr of York, now draws many visitors all year round. Its setting is perfect for Christmas banqueting and the Snowdrop Walk in February, now an annual event, is enjoyed by visitors and residents alike. (*Ron Loomes*)

Scorton village, 1953. In the shadow of a well-wooded hill, beyond which lie the desolate fells of Bleasdale, this stone-built village differed from the much older brick and clay villages of the Fylde plain. There was not a school until 1793. Although the Duke of Hamilton gave a plot of land, the villagers had to find the money to build it. The Roman Catholic church, not much more than 140 years old at the time of this photograph, replaced a tiny thatched church which served as the clogger's shop during the week. A law suit of 1622 revealed information about Scorton's tithe barn and tithe corn, the rights to which were let out at £43 per annum. Stonehead Farm, on the slopes of Catshaw beyond the village, and Fell End Farm, in the shadow of Harris End Farm, supplied milk and eggs and even today there are few shops in what was once called the 'metropolis of Wyresdale'. At weekends and holiday time this attractive village is very busy, being the gateway to the Bowland Fells and the famed Trough of Bowland through which the Lancashire witches passed on their way to trial and death in Lancaster Castle. The Women's Institute was a lively organisation in the village in the 1950s.

Ye Horn's Inn at Goosnargh, 1961. This public house has a long history as the date stone above the entrance attests – W.W.E. 1782. A well-known stopping place for coaches and horse-drawn wagonettes, a large set of stag's horns gave it the name and were mounted above the inn door, but these have long since rotted away.

Shepherd Jack Pye of Tarnbrook, a tiny hamlet in the Bleasdale Fells, 1962. One of five brothers of Gornall's Farm, for generations his family had been farmers and shepherds, some working for the Duke of Westminster. Jack had the misfortune to tread on an unexploded shell and his foot was badly damaged – the land was requisitioned by the Government during the war years and had been used as a training ground. In 1949 heath fires detonated more unspent ammunition. Not far from Jack's home is the Shepherds' Church. It is interesting to note that the confines of the old Fylde, i.e. Agermunderness, Hasmundernesse, Amounderness (archives over centuries show twelve variations of this name), reached from the sea to the fells.

The harvest festival at Little Eccleston, 1924. 'The Cornfield of Amounderness', as the Fylde was known, was well placed to lay on a splendid show at harvest time. In 1586 the historian Camden wrote of the 'File' or 'Field' being excellent for growing oats. The Domesday Book of 1086 recorded sixty-one villages but sixteen were sparsely populated and much of the area swamp. The nineteenth-century scheme to drain the mosses produced fertile growing country partly because the landowners united, allowing bricks and pipes to be made from the clay on their estates.

The sundial in the churchyard at Stalmine, 1962. This was probably adapted from an ancient preaching cross that had been introduced into the churchyard, perhaps a century previously. There was an underground passage linking the church with Stalmine Hall. At the hall they used to grow peaches on high brick walls warmed from below to ripen the fruits, which was considered revolutionary at the time. In the making of flats within the grounds of the hall in the early 1970s an ancient yew tree was illegally cut down.

An Elizabethan four-poster bed at Parrox Hall, Over Wyre, 1964. The house had a long history and is owned by the Elletson family. It also contains a black-bog oak case clock, some fine linen-fold panelling and tooled leather chairs, these last bought by Catherine de Braganza, wife of Charles II (who sent her to Parrox to recover her health). Open once a year for the benefit of the Gardeners' Benevolent Fund, the garden contains an old fig tree that fruits well.

Wrea Green Windmill, 1961. The windmill has been transformed into a luxury dwelling with landscaped grounds and appears to be receiving a visit from Father Christmas, better known as Dr Jonathan Ward, complete with reindeer and sack of presents. A four-storey tower mill, Wrea Green Windmill was working in 1770 but was fitted with a steam engine in 1860, which unfortunately later blew up and set the mill on fire. (*Dr Jonathan Ward*)

One of the tallest in the old Fylde, this was Pilling Windmill, built by Ralph Slater, millwright, and is seen here in the 1930s without its sails, which were smashed in a gale several years before or damaged by the installation of a steam engine. Eventually, like a number of others, it was renovated and converted to a dwelling house. The River Broadfleet flows in front of the mill.

ACKNOWLEDGEMENTS

Charles Ashton, Norman Boyes, Faith Bricher, Mrs K. Brown, Joan Currie, Ann and Christine Dickinson, Pauline Elvidge, Forsythe & Steele, Fylde Society of Model Engineers, Robert Gibson, Harry Grundy, Sheila Isherwood, Revd Martin Keighley, Lancashire Library, Mr W. Leadbetter, Leeds & District Traction Engine Club, Ron and Michael Loomes, Beryl McClellan, Poulton Historical Society, Revd Dr E.J. Rothwell, Ron Severs, Norman Short, Ron and Barbara Strachan, *West Lancashire Evening Gazette*, The Windmill Players, Cyril Wroe, Bill Yates. All photographs without credits are part of my own collection.